P50

PEEL EN[GINE]
EXTRAOR[DINARY]

Barry Edwards

CW00549708

Lily
Publications

THE STORY OF THE WORLD'S SMALLEST PRODUCTION CAR

Acknowledgements

This book is the result of many years of research. My involvement in the Manx Transport Heritage Museum in Peel in the early 2000s and that organisation's quest to find a P50 to bring home to the Island was the catalyst to the research.

During those years many people have been approached for information and all have willingly contributed, or pointed me in the right direction. To all of them, thank you. Thanks also to the following who have provided documents, photographs or memorabilia: Vic Bates, the late Cyril Cannell, Andrew Carter, Gordon Fitzgerald, Sam Knight and Chris Machin. Thanks also to Miles and Linda Cowsill of Lily Publications and their team: Nicola Green, Clare Price and Rosalind Stimpson for their patience during the production of the book and George Gelling, Neil Hanson and Ernie Leece for reading and correcting early versions of the text. Robert Stimpson provided information about patents.

Special thanks are due to the staff at the Manx National Heritage Library, Steve Jackson, Alan Jacobs, Wendy Thirkettle and Paul Weatherall for their willing assistance.

Grant Kearney deserves a special mention for his dedicated research and for allowing me unhindered access to his memorabilia collection and photographs. Claire Naylor, for her patience while we talk 'cars' often while enjoying the hospitality of the 'Toby Carvery' in Perth! Finally my wife Irene, for her patience during many evenings, while I sit glued to the computer.

Previous page: Members of Peel Engineering staff pose with the prototype P50 between two parked cars. Not only does this indicate the very light weight of the car but also its tiny size. (Manx National Heritage)

Right: A general view of the Peel Engineering factory from Mill Road. The higher part of the building was added specially to build 45ft long boats. The long lower shed is the main assembly area, and the house that Cyril Cannell lived in, in latter years, is visible behind. (Barry Edwards)

Introduction

Cyril Cannell started Peel Engineering in the late 1940s working with fibreglass, a new product that could be moulded into just about any shape and had the distinct advantage that it didn't rust.

Cyril pioneered many production processes and manufactured a wide range of products and many more experimental machines. A hovercraft was constructed as were a number of Go Karts. Anything that could be made in fibreglass was.

The first products were a sports car bodyshell and motorcycle fairings, many used in the TT races by some of the big names of that time. In the mid 1950s plans to market an innovative fibreglass car fell at the last hurdle.

Later this early attempt led to the development of the Peel cars, the now famous P50 and Trident but they were not the only types built. The Viking was a sports model designed to fit the Mini chassis, while other types fitted bigger chassis. Complete Mini and 1100 bodies were made in fibreglass and when tested in crash conditions performed better than their metal counterparts.

Sadly much of the original design drawings and notes were destroyed by Cyril himself, and it was unusual for him to talk about what he was thinking. However, much material has been retained by avid collectors and the memories of those who worked for Peel Engineering have provided much information about the Company and its wide range of products.

Plenty of leaflets and photographs do survive in the author's and other private collections, while some company information is available from official sources.

This book endeavours to tell the story of Peel Engineering throughout its existence, the various Peel Cars and the many other products.

I trust you will enjoy this fascinating story.

Barry Edwards
Ballasalla,
Isle of Man
October 2014

Several Peel Owners, former employees and indeed the author agreed that as part of the 50th celebrations, it would be appropriate to erect a plaque on the factory to record the innovation that emerged from Peel Engineering. Grant Kearney set about having a suitable plate manufactured, in fibreglass of course! Grant on the right and George Gelling, former workshop foreman, unveiled the plaque on Sunday 3 August 2014. (Barry Edwards)

A close up of the plaque now proudly displayed on the Peel Engineering factory. (Barry Edwards)

The Peel Engineering Story

Cyril Cannell

Cyril Cannell was born in Essex, the youngest of three sons, to a Manx-born schoolmaster from an old and respected Peel family. Cyril grew up in the Ilford and Romford area, and from an early age had an interest in transport and anything mechanical.

The Ford factory at Dagenham was just a short distance away and made a favourite school outing, not least because of the excellent tea provided.

Equally close by was the Great Eastern Railway Stratford locomotive works, where many locomotives were built and frequent visits here often included a footplate trip within the works.

Student days ended at the outbreak of WWII when Cannell joined the Royal Air Force and trained as an aircraft fitter and pilot. Despite failing the eyesight test, he emerged with an above average rating!

Much of 1941 was spent ferrying Hurricanes from Gibraltar to Malta from the aircraft carrier *Ark Royal*. Cannell then moved to the Air Training Corp in Rhodesia where he spent around two years as a multi-engine flying instructor. Cannell survived a serious engine fire while flying a Wellington bomber but suffered from periodic memory loss for many years, indeed nearly to retirement.

Shortly after the end of hostilities, the Cannell family acquired the long established Douglas Head Ferry Company, complete with the fleet of vessels; the largest licensed to carry 450 passengers. This business was developed originally in the Victorian era by William and Robert Knox, father and brother of the famous Manx artist Archibald Knox.

When not involved in ferry operations, time was spent at the Peel Shipyard building wooden boats and carrying out repairs. Early experimental work with fibreglass or GRP, led to the formation of Peel Engineering Limited, first registered on 31st December 1964.

Peel Engineering pioneered fibreglass vehicle body production and went on to manufacture a wide variety of motorcycle fairings and both complete and kit cars. The Company was dissolved by its directors on 10th May 1974.

Since that time Cyril Cannell has continued to design, and he holds a number of UK, Australian and US patents, the most recent for a new type of elevated railway, perhaps to link Douglas with Peel. It was also considered for the London 2012 Olympic site.

The Company

Peel Engineering, as it was to become, was started by Cyril Cannell in the late 1940s, the first products being boats. Cannell is reported to have travelled to America in the early 1950s to look at early fibreglass development. The company was one of the first to work with fibreglass, and initially occupied premises on the quay in Peel and traded as Viking Motors, later moving to Viking Works in Mill Road, Peel, to a building on the south side of the river Neb, originally occupied by Watson's Shipyard. The roof trusses for the workshop area came from RAF buildings at Andreas. The primary reason for the move was the purchase of Douglas Head Ferries by Cannell's father who planned to bring them round to Peel for maintenance. At the peak of production the Company employed around 40 people. It is known that some work was carried out in Hangar 292 at RAF Jurby Airfield for a period of about two years.

Peel Engineering Limited was registered as company number 001882C on 31st December 1964 with a capital of £5000 divided into £1 0s 0d shares. The Directors were Cyril Cannell of Victoria Terrace, Peel, and George Henry Kissack of Main Road, Crosby. The registered office was Viking Works. Advocates were Kelly, Moore, Hanson and Luft, Athol Street, Douglas.

In a transaction dated 10th November 1965, Cyril Cannell, now of Jurby, sold the goodwill and the full benefit of all of his own contracts to Peel Engineering Ltd and at the same time agreed to

Cyril Cannell captured having a joke with one of the visiting Peel owners in 2006.
(Barry Edwards)

lease Viking Works to the Company for £300 per annum, to be reviewed after five years.

A list of Plant, Machinery and loose tools in and about the premises included:

Trojan motor van licence number 768MN
12 Fairground motor boats
Glass-fibre Spraying Machine
Moulds for:
16ft Motorboat
10ft 6in Peelcraft Dinghy
8ft 6in Peelcraft Dinghy
Jinx
12 Motorcycle Fairing Moulds
2 Trident car moulds

A newspaper publicity image of a Peel TT Touring Fairing fitted to a Norman motorcycle. Photographed outside the Tynwald offices in Douglas. (Manx National Heritage)

A Fairing minus its windscreen but complete with its Peel Engineering maker's plate visible in the middle right of the picture. (Grant Kearney)

A Fairing, painted in a rather garish blue livery. The maker's plate can be clearly seen. (Grant Kearney)

There was a similar transaction from George Henry Kissack on the same day but it only included the sale of various tools to the company.

George Henry Kissack died on 16th March 1972 and was succeeded by his wife Eileen May Kissack as a Director of the Company, her appointment taking effect on 3rd November 1972.

Eileen May Kissack resigned her directorship on 25th November 1973 and was succeeded by Alice Victoria Maud Cannell on 30th November 1973.

The agreement to dissolve the company was made by its directors on 10th May 1974. The actual dissolution taking place on 29th August 1974, with notices of dissolution appearing in the *Isle of Man Courier* and *Examiner*, both dated 6th September 1974.

The Products of Peel Engineering

The Company produced a very wide range of products during its time but the exact order of development of the various products remains unclear. Research in the local press has dated some of the products while the timing of others remains unconfirmed. It is quite possible that some 'one offs' were made, about which nothing is really known, so the following may not therefore be exhaustive.

The product descriptions that follow are in no particular order but are dated where enough evidence of production dates has been discovered.

Ford 10 Chassis Body (Sports Car Body)

One of the first products was a sports car body to fit the 7'6" wheelbase Ford 8/10 or a Morris 8

A Peel TT Touring Fairing in need of some serious restoration, again though with its maker's badge clearly visible. A bit of TLC and a new coat of paint and it will look as good as new. (Grant Kearney)

chassis. A simple moulded one piece body, it required the purchaser to provide some internal framing for support. It looked similar to that later sold as the P1000.

A director from the Ford Motor Company came to the Island wanting Peel Engineering to supply GRP sports car bodies to Ford for them to produce and market a sports car. This sadly came to nothing after the Isle of Man Government turned down Cannell's request for funding to enlarge the factory, to accommodate the production of the large numbers of car bodies required by Ford.

A report in the *Isle of Man Examiner* of 21st August 1953 talked about the plant preparing for production of the sports car body. The article went on to say that if you want a car badly enough and

are prepared to go back to your Meccano days, you can put one together for £150 0s 0d.

The prototype had taken three months to develop and the production car was to be available in red, blue, green and cream, and would cost around £70. Designed to enable the serious enthusiast to build a two or three-seater sports car, using a popular chassis from a Ford 8 or 10, the lightweight body allowed exceptional performance.

An added advantage was to be the light-weight 'Coupé' top section, being developed by Peel Engineering, which would just clip on to make an all-weather car.

A further report in the Isle of Man Examiner of 21st January 1955 talked about the forthcoming Trade fair at the Palace Ballroom, Douglas, where

A close up of a makers plate, all fairings had numbers prefixed with 'B'. The company produced around 25 fairings per month. (Grant Kearney)

80 traders were expected to exhibit. Peel Engineering were in attendance with their Manx made two-seater sports car body, produced by brothers Douglas and Cyril Cannell of Peel and Henry Kissack of Crosby.

Manx body in fibreglass

The use of plastics and fibreglass for the construction of complete body shells, and such parts as luggage locker lids, is slowly increasing as more knowledge of manufacturing methods are obtained. Apart from the very light weight as compared with that of a similar body of steel or aluminium panels, two advantages of this fibreglass body are its ability to take a good paint finish and its resistance to damage.

The Peel Engineering Company of The Shipyard, Peel, Isle of Man, are producing a body shell of fibreglass which is suitable for mounting on Ford Eight and Ten chassis. The top profile takes the shape of a continuous shallow curve with slight protuberances over the wheels. The designers have in mind that the customer is to carry out a certain amount of work himself, and an alternative front section can be supplied with headlamps faired into the wings and the frontal area left without any air intake opening, so that the individual may cut it to whatever shape he chooses.

The length of the body shell is 12ft, with an interior width of 4ft 7in, while the approximate weight of the shell is 56lb. The price of the moulding is £72 and a 'clip-on' coupé top is in the development stage.

From the appearance viewpoint this type of construction gains enormously over some of the bodywork to be seen on 'specials', which sometimes look as if the constructor has thrown a few panels on to the framework from a great distance!

Template drawings are supplied with the shell and Peel Engineering Co. are able to undertake modifications to the design illustrated.

Peel Fairings

The first Peel Fairing was made in 1952 for an

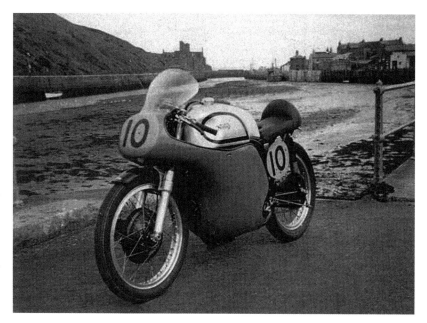

A Mark 1 Racing style Fairing fitted to a Norton Motorcycle and photographed alongside the quay in Peel. (George Gelling)

Australian over for the TT Races, a full 'dustbin'. The Company was the first to produce fibreglass racing fairings.

Various other shapes were produced for different bikes including one for Geoff Duke who asked for a Dolphin style to fit a Manx Norton. In conjunction with Geoff, the 'Dolphin' fairing was tested and further developed on the Island with some additional testing done in Monza. A full production version was offered in 1957 and latterly there were a number of different 'Dolphin' Style fairings. The 'Dustbin' was also manufactured with a PVC screen and aluminium beading round the edge, intended for road bikes. Local racer W Prynne's bike (himself a Peel Engineering employee) had a 'Dustbin' fairing. Fairings for BMW bikes were also produced.

The Manx Green Final (a local sports newspaper) of 26th April 1958 reported that Geoff Duke had won at Silverstone riding a Norton 350 fitted with a Peel Dolphin streamlined fairing in light blue and that it was expected that Peel would be manufacturing the fairing to be used by Geoff for his BMW being prepared for his entry into the 1958 TT races.

Peel Engineering developed a way of blowing bubbles with Perspex. This process was used to make screens for fairings and the domes for the Trident. Here we see the process about to start, the warming of the Perspex sheet between two sets of heaters. (Manx National Heritage)

Further development brought the cheaper touring model and later the Jet black coloured fairing incorporating a rectangular Cibie Headlamp, almost twice as powerful as an ordinary 7" British lamp without using any more power.

R C Duggan, writing in *The Motor Cycle* of August 1957, recounts that he and his friend W. Prynne, both Manx motorcyclists, were among the first to try Peel Fairings. Duggan had an A.J.S Twin and Prynne a Norton Dominator 88.

Interestingly both riders found that their bikes were less sensitive to cross winds with the fairings fitted, the only problem experienced was the reduced steering lock. They both enthused about the protection offered to the rider by the fairing, indeed noting that gloves were not needed in normal conditions. Dave Williams won the 1964 Southern 100 using a MK3 Peel Fairing with enclosed handlebars, and Selwyn Griffiths won the 1964 Senior Manx Grand Prix. Many of the big names of the TT rode with Peel Fairings, Mike Hailwood, Mike Duff, Bob McIntyre to name a few.

The *Isle of Man Examiner* of 22nd January 1959 reported that Peel Engineering had received an enquiry from the USA asking for a quote to manufacture and deliver 138 Fairings, the

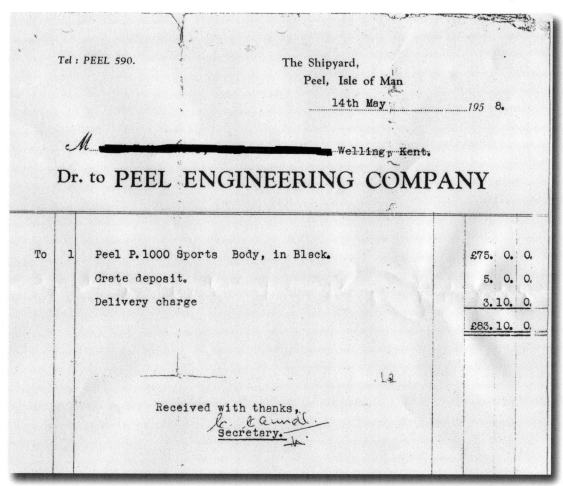

Tel : PEEL 590.

The Shipyard,
Peel, Isle of Man

14th May 195 8.

M ▬▬▬▬▬▬▬▬▬ Welling, Kent.

Dr. to PEEL ENGINEERING COMPANY

To	1	Peel P.1000 Sports Body, in Black.	£75.	0.	0.
		Crate deposit.	5.	0.	0.
		Delivery charge	3.10.	0.
			£83.10.	0.

Received with thanks,
Secretary.

An interesting invoice for a P1000 body for a customer in Kent. The phone number would now be 6 digits, the address would include a postcode, the finance would be in decimal and the whole thing no doubt produced on a computer! The car had obviously been painted for the customer in black. (Authors Collection)

THE PEEL
"T.T. TOURING" FAIRING

Type B.M.W. (Suitable for fitting to B.M.W. R50, R60 and R69 machines)

A

MUST

FOR ALL

B.M.W.

OWNERS

<small>Photo by permission of 'Motor Cycling'</small>

MORE

SPEED . . .

COMFORT . . .

WEATHER
PROTECTION !

PRODUCED BY

PEEL ENGINEERING COMPANY

THE SHIPYARD, PEEL, ISLE OF MAN :: Telephone: PEEL 590

Designed for fitting to BMW machines exclusively, the Fairing provides almost complete enclosure at the front with minimum opening round the fork legs, giving excellent weather protection. Cooling air is ducted round the cylinders, any moisture which may be carried through is deflected downwards, the top part of the duct forms a useful pocket for carrying gloves, maps, etc.

TYPE	Dolphin pattern.
MATERIAL	Best quality glassfibre with steel reinforced attachment points. Transparent Cobex Windscreen for durability with alloy edging.
CONSTRUCTION	Produced in two main sections, allowing the Fairing to be fitted to the machine quickly without removing the front wheel assembly.
DIMENSIONS	Length : 38½ inches. Width : 23 inches. Height (to top of standard 18″ Windscreen): 28½″ Weight : 14 lbs. complete.

AVAILABLE in Primer £21 0 0
      in Standard colours Black, Silver Grey,
         Post Office Red, Riviera Blue £22 10 0
      in Special colours or Duo-tone £23 10 0

WHEN ORDERING DIRECT ---- Send remittance including carriage charge. If you can collect the Fairing (uncrated), from your nearest Airport served by B.E.A. or Silver City (Northern) Airlines, this will be 10/-; otherwise the Fairing will be despatched per Passenger Parcels Service in a wooden crate, the carriage cost being 20/-. A deposit of £3 is required for the crate, which is refunded immediately it is returned to us in good condition, carriage paid.

N.M.P. Ltd.

A Peel Engineering fairing leaflet promoting the TT Touring Fairing for fitting to various BMW motorcycles. The prices make interesting reading, a fairing for just over £1.0s.0d.
(Authors Collection)

handsome safety shells used by 76% of the 1958 TT riders. Fairings had already been supplied to 17 countries.

The early fairings had bought-in windscreens but, following closure of the supplying business, Peel Engineering quickly learned how to make windscreens. A steel welded box lined with cooker elements in the bottom and over the top was heated up in the morning, and it was possible to blow between 30 and 40 complete screens a day. A simple wire showed how far to blow each one, any finishing and cutting being completed after the shaping. Later the Bubble for the Trident was made in the same way, using temperatures up to 120 degrees to get the best results.

The fairings products were eventually sold to Ivory Plastics in Luton. All stock and the moulds along with fittings for the various bike types were shipped. A wide range of specific drawings were prepared and, as part of the deal, Peel Engineering was to receive royalties on all subsequent sales.

Peel Girls' Part in TT

This was the title of an article in the *Isle of Man Daily Times* of 13th June 1961. The article describes how TT week was a good time for Peel Engineering to invite a local Woman's magazine to visit the factory.

'Many of the top riders have fairings manufactured by Peel, and the major part of that production is handled by two girls; Miss Celia Hall and Miss Edith Quayle, both aged 17. The girls describe how they feel proud when watching the races and seeing 'their' fairings whizzing round'.

The Hovercraft

In the early 1960s the Company produced a hovercraft, powered by a Triumph twin ex-War Department 500cc engine. It had two seats in the open and although it worked the project never got any further. Former employees remember seeing this 'flying without a skirt', however, a hovercraft will not work without one. It may have 'flown' with the

Another fairing leaflet showing a wide variety of fairings for different manufacturers of motorcycle. (Authors Collection)

The Hovercraft being 'land tested'. Cyril Cannell stands chatting to Helen Costain, while Henry Kissack inspects the power supply for the craft. The picture is taken outside the former Mill building in Mill Road, across the river from the main factory area. (Manx National Heritage)

flexible part of the skirt omitted and hovered with just the rigid backing.

The Isle of Man Daily Times of 17th January 1961 included an article about the hovercraft, suggesting that the Manx-built single-seater craft was nearing completion at the Peel Engineering works. It had already 'hovered' 6 inches above the ground and would have a top speed of 35mph. The prototype would be on display at the Manx Trades Fair at the end of the month. Cyril Cannell and Henry Kissack had given the project two years of intensive experiment and were keen to finalise the design.

The machine was 9ft long and 5ft wide, the main platform containing the outer and inner skins which cause the craft to 'hover'. Forward and cornering control is provided by a lever that moves the position of the vents.

The main fan was of a centrifugal type, constructed completely in fibreglass, and provided headaches for its designers. Each blade had to be moulded with extreme accuracy to provide balance when operating.

Cyril Cannell pointed out that being made completely of fibreglass it weighed just 220lb. This was demonstrated when 3 men picked it up and carried it outside to allow the picture to be taken.

Power was provided by a twin-cylinder Triumph motorcycle engine of 500cc capacity. The engine was laid horizontally at the rear of the craft with a belt making the final drive to the fan, itself located slightly to the rear of centre of the craft. The front part of the body was a seat, and if a suitable bigger engine could be sourced, it could be adapted to carry two passengers.

Following a visit to the London Boat Show in January 1961, and the potential availability of a larger power unit, the designers envisaged a ten-seater version in the near future. They had identified many uses for such a craft around the Island, including from Peel Beach to the Breakwater.

A land version was also under consideration.

Peel Gyrojet

Powered by a British Anzani engine the prototype

was tested in Peel bay. A drawing of the Peel Gyrojet shows it similar in appearance to the Hovercraft but operating more like a jet ski.

Fibreglass Duck

This was an invention by Cyril Cannell, whereby a tube was installed round the propeller of motorised vessels to improve the efficiency of the propeller. This is known as the ducted fan principle.

Boats

Peel Engineering produced a variety of boats, dinghies and canoes. The bigger vessels were known as 'Inshoreman' and 'Offshoreman'.

The 'INSHOREMAN' Motorboat *(Designers - Burness, Corlett and Partners, Naval Architects)*

This roomy 16ft or 18ft motorboat was designed on the most modern lines, with particular attention to ease of propulsion and good sea-keeping qualities. Ample flare was provided forward to keep the boat dry, together with a transom proportioned for safety in following seas. The design complied with M.O.T (UK Ministry of Transport) Regulations as a 'B' Class lifeboat to carry up to thirteen persons, and could be supplied to this specification if required.

Twin keels were provided for additional stability, and to enable the craft to stand upright in harbour without the necessity for unsightly 'legs'. They also

Another of the many products to emerge from the factory were these propeller ducted fan housings. Designed to increase the power output of a propeller, the modification could be applied to almost any vessel. (George Gelling)

A close up of the power unit and fan as installed in the prototype Hovercraft. The ingenuity of getting all the bits to fit into the space available is clearly evident. The engine is a triumph twin. (Manx National Heritage)

gave considerable protection to the propeller.

Whilst an inboard marine engine (Stuart Turner 8 H.P. or Lister 9 or 13 H.P. Diesel) was generally recommended as standard equipment, provision could be made for an outboard motor to be mounted in a 'well', giving the advantages of protection to the motor, easy access to same from the boat, and occupying less space than an inboard motor.

The construction was of best quality glass-reinforced plastic for long life and ease of maintenance.

A detachable Cabin Top was available for those who required shelter, and internal fittings, toilet, stove, bunks etc, could be installed if required.

Dimensions
Length Overall: 16ft or 18ft
Beam: 6'2"
Draft: 2'3"

Price
Hull complete with PVC Fender, Cleats, Mooring lines, buoyancy etc. 16ft @ £280, 18ft @ £330

Engine and installation
Stuart Turner 4 H.P. with reduction gear £150 + £30 installation. Petrol.
Stuart Turner 8 H.P. direct drive £172 + £30 installation.
Stuart Turner 8 H.P. with reduction gear £195 +

The development of the Hovercraft was never completed but, clearly Cyril Cannell was already working on the next phase of development. The Peel Gyrojet would have provided an interesting vehicle for Island residents.
(Manx National Heritage)

Peel Engineering Isle of Man.

Peel GYROJET

£30 installation.
G.M. Seawitch 9 H.P. with variable pitch propeller
£130 + £30 installation. Diesel.
Lister 9 H.P. or 13 H.P. from £250 + £45
installation.

All above with electric starting at extra cost.

Delivery was free to any part of the Isle of Man.
Terms of Business: 10% deposit with order, 50% on
completion of hull, balance on acceptance of boat
prior to delivery.

The 'OFFSHOREMAN' Motorboat

The Peel Offshoreman was a 60/40 motor sailer,
single screw, and designed with keel rake, divided
into four main compartments, comprising of a
forecastle, galley and bathroom space, engine room
and wheel house space and after cabin.

The ship has the following dimensions:

Length Overall	33' 0"
Length on waterline.	28' 10"
Beam moulded amidships.	9' 5"
Depth moulded amidships.	6' 0"
Maximum draft aft.	4' 6"
Maximum draft amidships.	4' 3"
Normal Operational draft:	
Aft	4' 3"
Amidships	3' 11"
Thames Measurement approx.	11 tons.
Ballast moulded in	3 to 4 tons.

The hull was of glass-reinforced plastic construction
of 10-12 oz. per square ft GRP laminate with semi-

Although famous for its cars, Peel Engineering built fair quantities of boats. Here we see a well used 'Inshoreman' on the factory site in August 2014. The vessel still has its Peel Engineering badge and makers plate showing production number D567. (Barry Edwards)

Through the years Peel Engineering produced a wide range of products. These toy boats were among them. The condition shows that they had been lying on a shelf of the factory for many years before being discovered during a clear out. (Barry Edwards)

The lake behind the Peel Brickworks, the office of which now forms the accommodation for the Manx Transport Heritage Museum, the home of a preserved P50, was ideal for sailing the Peel produced pleasure craft. Here three young people put one of the Peel built craft through its paces. (Manx National Heritage)

Peel Engineering produced a number of boats for the Onchan Park boating lake. Boat number 9 is seen here being put through its paces by two gentlemen who hardly seem dressed for such activity!
(Manx National Heritage)

flexible gel coat. Resin used was of the water resistant type such as Stypol 921 and all fibreglass was 'E' type.

The deck was to be moulded in a similar way to the hull.

The deck house construction shown on the general arrangement consisted of 3/4" teak faced marine plywood sides, fronts and backs, with 9/16" coach roof tops moulded from 3/16" marine ply. Windows were to be heavy quality Perspex, held in position by P.V.C. glazing strip surrounds. Front windows to be of armour-plate glass.

A double cabin was to be incorporated to have bunks constructed of GRP, with locker space underneath and with a light at the head of each bunk.

The wheelhouse was to be raised, as in the general arrangement with an 18" diameter steering wheel , and a galley to be arranged forward of the wheelhouse to starboard as shown. This was to contain a Henderson or Whale type bilge Pump suitably located, a suitable stainless steel or GRP sink as shown with hand pump from the fresh water tank, with an alcohol stove fitted forward of this for cooking purposes.

The forward cabin was to contain two bunks with

'Waste not want not' was clearly the motto of the company. Here some 50 years after being used to manufacture parts, this fibreglass mould now serves as a flower pot in the grounds surrounding the factory. (Barry Edwards)

A detailed drawing of a Peel
Engineering Fishing Vessel,
showing finished layout and
position of the power unit and
all internal fittings.
(Authors Collection)

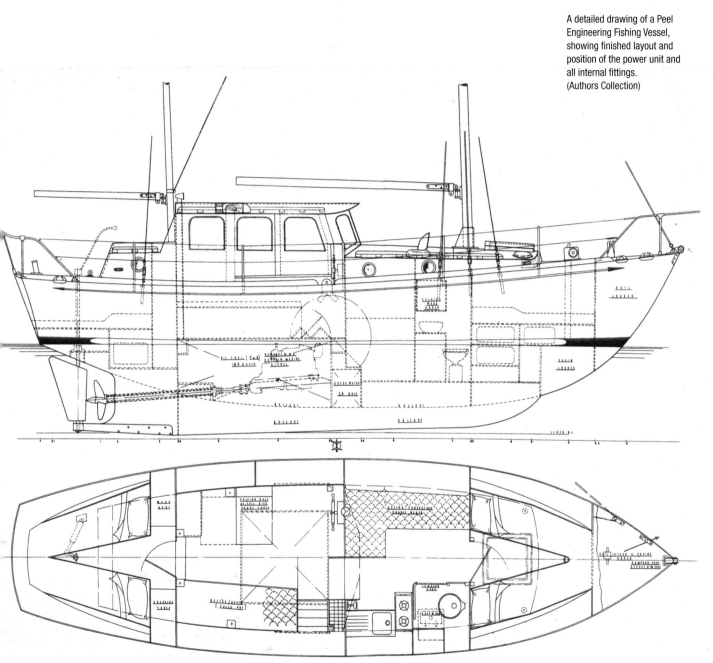

PEEL ENGINEERING LIMITED. VIKING WORKS. PEEL, ISLE OF MAN. Tel: PEEL 590

with berth lights over each and locker space would be incorporated.

Peel Marine Craft

The Peel Engineering range of small craft were all produced in the highest quality glass-fibre material and embody many years of experience in this field. In the composition of the material only fillers of the proper type and quantity are used, the resultant laminate closely following the recommended Admiralty specifications, and could be relied upon to give great durability and service.

Each craft was designed specifically for their intended purpose, under the exacting conditions which are found in Manx waters. Built-in buoyancy tanks were an integral part of each hull, and were of sufficient capacity to give an ample reserve of flotation even with the craft completely flooded.

Peel craft could be supplied in any colour to order and required little maintenance. If repairs should ever have be necessary, they were very simply carried out.

'Peelcraft' Dinghy 8'0" x 4'2" beam x 15" depth moulded.

This little boat was light enough to be easily handled and could be carried on top of a car or on a small trailer, and could be carried by one person if required. Even so, it could accommodate 3-4

The Manxcar chassis as removed or probably before fitting to the body. (George Gelling)

persons, and be propelled at a useful speed with an outboard motor of up to 1½hp.

Price - £45 0s 0d, complete with oars, rowlocks, mooring lines etc. Weight 1cwt.

'Peelcraft' Dinghy 10'6" length x 4'6" beam x 19" depth moulded.

This was an excellent small sea-boat weighing just 1½ cwt. approx, and proved itself for fishing and all round general purpose use in local waters. An outboard motor of 2½hp. gave a speed of around 5mph fully loaded with 4 persons. Alternatively, the design could accommodate an inboard unit if preferred. A 12'6" version was also available.

Price — £90 0s 0d, complete with oars, rowlocks, mooring lines, rubber fend-off, etc.

Alternatively, as above, less rubber fend-off - £85 0s 0d.

The Company could undertake the construction of larger craft to customer specific requirements.

The *Isle of Man Examiner* of 30th April 1959 reported that Peel Engineering had displayed a 10'6" dinghy at the Manx Trader Fair in January. Capable of carrying 5 persons the dinghy had expanding foam in the construction to improve buoyancy. The same article reported that the company employed 14 staff.

The *Mona's Herald,* of 27th January 1959, reported of the Trades Fair that Sir Ralph Stevenson (A member of Legco 1955-1970 and Captain of the Parish of Arbory 1963-1976) examined the streamlined fibreglass dinghy made by Peel Engineering, and described it as the best exhibit in the fair.

Isle of Man Examiner on 4th August 1960 reported that a gala event held in Peel was a great success, with the added novelty, Peel Engineering loaned a fibreglass dinghy to be used in the balloon race but the over enthusiasm of the youngsters led to it being withdrawn.

The Manxcar

In 1955 Peel Engineering, having produced car

bodies and parts, motorcycle fairings and boat hulls, decided the time was right to move into kit car production. The end of the War had seen a shortage of cars in the UK as most of those built were reserved for export. The Manxman, as it was known, could be purchased fully assembled or in kit form, thus avoiding the purchase tax levied on assembled vehicles.

The Manxman was a three-wheeler (two front, one rear wheel) on a light tubular T type chassis with a fibreglass panelled body. It was driven by a British Anzani twin-cylinder two-stroke fan cooled engine of 250 or 350cc capacity.

Initially a BSA stationary engine was trialled but found to be unsuitable. A prototype was shown to staff from *Motor Cycling* magazine during the June 1955 TT races and again in January 1956, but objections from the then UK Customs and Excise meant that purchase tax might have been payable, making the project unviable and so it was abandoned.

The vehicle was reportedly going to be available with either a 4-speed forward or 3-speed forward and one reverse gear box, and was started electrically via a 12-volt Siba Dynastart. Wheel size was 8" diameter and a 7" brake with locked hydraulic system was included, each wheel being independently sprung. The car was built to cruise at 35 to 40mph with a maximum speed of 50mph, and was advertised as able to achieve around 90mpg.

The doors were pivoted in the bottom rear corner and lifted flush with the side of the car through 90 degrees. A third door gave access to a flat 16-cu ft boot space that included a trap door for access to the engine, and had a foot well fitted to allow two children to be carried behind the main seats. The vehicle had hammock style seats, similar to that later fitted into the P50.

Overall dimensions were; Wheelbase 5'6", Track 3'11", Length 7'6", Height 4'4", Weight 4.5 cwt. The complete car supplied assembled would have cost £299 10s 0d.

The prototype vehicle was registered UMN 10, the registration description being a three-wheeler saloon with four seats in red, both the chassis and

engine numbers showing as 10. Registered to C Cannell and G H Kissack, trading as Peel Engineering for trade purposes on 17th September 1955. The registration was cancelled on 1st October 1962.

The original name 'Manxman' conflicted with a motorcycle produced by Excelsior and so would have been 'Manxcar' if production had gone ahead.

The *Isle of Man Examiner* of 20th January 1956 reported that the slogan 'We give you the parts, you build the car' was that used by Cyril Cannell and Henry Kissack, who firmly believed that that after three years development they had produced the

This view of the Manxcar shows the hatchback style rear door and the sliding guide for the front driver's door.
(George Gelling)

The Manxcar, like all Peel products was innovative. This view shows the lifting door that when open would partially cover the rear window.
(George Gelling)

A formal press picture of the prototype P50.
(Manx National Heritage)

cheapest, lightest and safest three-wheel car ever invented. Available complete or in kit form, the kit would have been about 50% cheaper.

The report went on to say that the residents of Peel had become used to various contraptions being tested in and around the town over the past few years.

The *Mona's Herald* of 7th February 1956 further reported that arrangements were expected to be completed in order for production to begin. Enquiries had been received from all over the world.

Peel 1000

The Peel 1000, based on the Austin Healey design, was a self-supporting body, so designed to avoid the use of an internal frame. It has a 7'6" wheelbase. It came in three sections, front with bonnet lid and dashboard, double skinned doors incorporating built in pockets, and the rear section including the boot lid. The whole thing could be packed into a 5'0" cube.

Quite a number of these bodies were produced, many shipped away in crates, but one is known to survive on the Island. Cyril Cannell had a P1000 on a BSA 10hp chassis.

An advertisement in the *Autocar* of 10th April 1959 shows the body available for £75 and an optional hard top for an additional £20.

P50 Prototype and Test Chassis

The P50 was designed and built by Cyril Cannell and Henry Kissack, and launched at the 1962 Earl's Court Motorcycle Show, using the concept car produced to evaluate sizes and possible features. This vehicle was never motorised. The overall dimensions are 4'4" long, 3'3" wide and 3'10" high. Cyril Cannell once referred to the prototype as the P55 in a conversation with the press, but officially it was always the P50. This vehicle was sold into preservation on 16th May 1974.

Prior to the manufacture of the prototype body shell, a chassis was being tested on the Island with the engine driving the single front wheel. Despite

being more stable, the wheel arrangement was reversed for the production P50s, supposedly because it was easier to build the car with the twin wheels at the front.

The P50

The prototype P50 led the way to the production P50s, but with some major differences. The wheel arrangement was reversed, the production cars having the single wheel at the rear rather than at the front. The P50 was the first production car manufactured on the Island, and the smallest ever production car in the world. The smallest ever record is argued to have been lost to the Brutsch Mopetta built in Germany. Peel enthusiasts will agree this is not the case as recent research shows that, in terms of 'cube', the P50 is smaller. The P50 design drawings were all done on a plastic material that over the years disintegrated and so, sadly, no drawings remain. Early promotional material in 1962 suggested that using a P50 was cheaper than walking.

There was no chassis, the front and rear axle assemblies being constructed of welded tubular steel, and the vehicle was powered by an engine from Zweirad Union, part of the German D.K.W. Group. (Zweirad translates to 'Two Wheels'. DKW is Dampf Kraft Wagen where Kraft Wagen translates to 'Steam Driven Car'. The DKW factory was in Nurmburg, West Germany, now part of the Audi Group.) This single-cylinder 49cc 6600rpm fan cooled two-stroke produced 4.2bhp using a petrol mixture of 25:1. Despite the 25:1 petrol-oil mixture requirement some owners put neat petrol in their cars, even though the fuel cap doubled as the oil measure, causing some problems for the Company. The engine, situated to the right side, was separated from the interior of the car by ample thickness of fibreglass. A one and a half gallon fuel tank with internally visible level was fitted. The car was started by a hand lever in the floor and contained a three-speed forward gearbox with final drive via an enclosed chain to the rear wheel. A chrome handle on the rear acted as reverse, the driver simply picking the car up and turning it round. The gear selection was made by a quadrant mounted lever on the steering column and had forward and aft movement only. The car had a maximum speed of 40mph and was capable of 100mpg. The five inch wheels were fitted with Avon 3.50 x 5 Moto Cart tyres and were all interchangeable. A compensated foot brake operated on the two front wheels while the handbrake used the single rear wheel. All brakes were connected by easily adjustable cables. The three standard pedals were actually core plugs welded to metal arms. Suspension was provided by fully independent telescopic coil spring units with nylon bushes. The car had an un-laden weight of 130lbs.

The December 1964 issue of *Garage News* magazine quoted the road tax as being £6 10s 0d and that trafficators are fitted. It also talks about the ingenious windscreen washer, worked by squeezing a plastic bottle full of liquid!

All lights are powered by the battery, which in turn is charged by alternator. The rectifier made by Mullard (now part of Philips) is known as a silicon Diode Rectifier, and is smaller than a sixpence in diameter. The vehicle had no speedometer or indeed any other instruments. The seat was a sprung rubber suspended hammock style on a tubular frame. In 1963 the vehicle retailed at £199 10s 0d although £179 16s 8d was also quoted.

The *Small Car Magazine* asked the UK Ministry of Transport if it was legal to market a car with no Speedometer. The answer came back, 'Yes', 'a three-wheeler weighing less than 8cwt was classed as a motorcycle, and a motorcycle of less than 100cc did not need a speedometer'.

The body was of fibreglass, with a door on one side only, but was not made in the conventional way by laying matting and then covering with resin. Instead, Cyril Cannell devised a method of chopping the glass fibre strands into 1.5 inch lengths in a special mechanical cutter, situated between two spray nozzles, resin coming from one and hardener from the other. The suction caused by these sucks the chopped strands, thus spraying all three components together. Using this method a complete car body can be sprayed in just 10 minutes. The resin, or hardener, was made up of 14 ingredients and was supplied by Scott Bader of Wellingborough and/or Freeman Chemicals on the Wirral, who interestingly still supply some of the products likely to have been supplied to Peel Engineering. The patterns were made in plaster on a wooden frame; the moulds were fibreglass supported by a metal frame. The moulds were coated with a special wax imported from America; up to 100 bodies were possible from each application of wax. Cannell's method is now widely used in the GRP industry and is widely referred to as the Chopped Strand Matting process.

The first cars had flat rear panels down to the mounting place for the rear lamps, later ones have a web above the rear lights. This was due to a change in production method. Early cars were produced by painting the gel coat onto the inside of the mould and then the fibreglass was sprayed onto it. Later models were made starting with a PVC sheet heated in a similar way to the fairing windscreens and then pulled into shape by motors and chains over a former. The fibreglass was then sprayed onto the inside of the PVC sheet.

Early examples also differed in that they had a steel anti-roll bar and higher exhaust; later cars had the anti-roll bar moulded in during the construction of the fibreglass. The chain race cover provided the

An early picture of a P1000 finished in what appears to be white. These vehicles would have varied from each other as individual builders used different parts to complete them. (Grant Kearney)

A complete P1000 body clearly showing the various different sections. The stylish design is very evident from this view. (Grant Kearney)

A complete P1000 body being
prepared for preservation.
(Grant Kearney)

same protection on the nearside.

The car was available in Daytona White, Dragon Red, Capri Blue and Sunshine Yellow, and at least one picture survives showing a two-tone car. Everything possible was made 'in-house', the rubber corner protection is boat fender, as used on dinghies, the side lamps Lucas, and the badges were made on a hot foil printer. The steering column cover showing the gear positions was also printed in-house.

Current owners tell of a number of variations with each vehicle indicating a very much hand-built and finished production line.

The car can be rolled on its side when a wheel change is required and only takes about 2 minutes to wash!

About 55 cars were produced between 1962 and 1965, the first cars sold went off-Island. P50s were sent to other parts of the world including America, where the Bureau of Transportation Inspector rolled the car down an embankment, but as he escaped without a scratch, he passed the car as suitable for use immediately.

King William's College on the Island had a P50 presented to them by the Reverend Parkes, to assist in teaching mechanics. It was a white vehicle (documents show the colour as red) first registered on 28th March 1964 as 9504 MN. It had chassis number D539 and engine number E804 16004683. This vehicle still exists in private ownership on the Island.

A visitor to the Manx Transport Heritage Museum in Peel, who was a former employee of Newcastle General Hospital, gave some information about a P50 that, following conversion to electric propulsion by Smiths Electric Vehicles of Newcastle in about 1962, was used in and around the Hospital.

Extract from the P50 road test by Bruce Cox of 'Motorcycle Mechanics' (Date unknown):
'Summing up the Peel it is fair to say that as a touring vehicle it has little potential, but that is not what the manufacturers intend it to be used as. They have built the Peel for round-town work and for that it is ideal. A housewife going into town for her shopping or a businessman commuting into the city centre would have a job to find anything more suitable for their purpose than the Peel. It is quite fast enough for city streets, has good brakes, is economical, easy to park and highly manoeuvrable.'

Isle of Man Examiner, 8th November 1962:
The *Examiner* included an article in their edition dated 8th November 1962 that carried the headline, 'From Peel to Earl's Court — Island makes smallest car!' The price to be £149 10s 0d.

The reporter, Harry Clarke, had been to the works to drive the P50. Mr Clarke reported:

'The makers feel that this vehicle will meet the demand of 1000s of buyers who require a car offering the economy and convenience of a scooter or a small motorcycle, but with complete protection from the elements and providing simple but adequate space for parcels, clothing, tools and such like!

The outstanding features include an easy starting mechanism not dependant on electricity. Adequate lighting is provided with Wipac side and rear lamps and headlamps complete with dipping mechanism. A parking switch is also provided.

It has a windscreen wiper and washer and an important item is the 'intalock' seating in rubber suspended, anatomically correct for persons of any stature.

The controls have been arranged in conventional position - clutch, brake and accelerator pedals and a hand gear change. There is a simple choke control system fitted with an auto off device.

The Varley battery is kept charged by an AC generator through a rectifier unit, to provide ample road and parking lights.

This little motor car has been tested over the famous TT mountain course and it climbed up round the Gooseneck and the Mountain section of the course very comfortably, using its easily changed 3-speed gearbox.

The P50 will be at the centre of the Company's stand, alongside a large selection of motorcycle fairings, at the show with secretary Miss Helen Cowell on hand to take orders.'

Isle of Man Examiner Road Test report, 20th February 1964:

The P50 reportedly came through a trade journal road test with flying colours, and the positive reports led to increased output of the cars and hence a reduction in the price from £199 18s 9d to £179 17s 11d.

The actual report showed that the car was given a full-blown try-out by an expert, and included a drive through the streets of London. 'One of the journal's drivers was in a large saloon car, the other in the P50. In a 15 mile drive from a Two-Stroke Vehicle Showroom in Stanmore to Fleet Street, on a Friday afternoon, the P50 covered the 15 miles 30 minutes quicker than the saloon, due mainly to its ability to get through narrow gaps in queues of traffic'.

The report continued:

'Because of the low weight, stopping was very rapid and skid free. The front brakes were very effective and gave the driver confidence to use the machine's tiny dimensions to full effect in the heavy traffic. To test how easily the car would turn over, it was driven round in ever decreasing circles on a gravelled car park and it was difficult to even raise a wheel'.

The report concluded:

'Our short experience (in one hour's driving) left us most impressed - we enjoyed its lively performance and extraordinary abilities in congested traffic'.

One wonders what it would be like to drive a P50 in London traffic today.

The following extract is from a column by Glyn Roberts in 'Motorcycle Scooter and Three Wheeler Mechanics' of April 1964.

'Motorcyclists, in which term I include all riders and drivers of powered two and three-wheelers, have always known of the advantages of their chosen form of transport and have found no difficulty in understanding that if you were to remove from the roads the mobile road blocks - the buses, and those five and six-seater cars with only one occupant – the driver, and place the people so carried, on or in two-and three-wheelers, then you would give our town road systems a traffic capacity increased perhaps by as much as 200 per cent.

Everyone with whom I discuss the subject admits the convenience and speed of the bike, the low cost and manoeuvrability of the three-wheeler. Why then don't more people use them? The average chap won't use a two-wheeler because it is often wet and nearly always cold, dressing-up 'is a damned nuisance', and that's enough for the girl friend, too. In the case of the three-wheeler the little car is low powered, comparatively expensive and needs as much room on the road as a four-wheeler.

One of these days someone will come up with the answer. Maybe it will be something after the style of the Peel, a tiny one-seater which will get through the gaps as easily as a solo, and for which special parking facilities may eventually be allowed. Perhaps, on the other hand, it will be a two-wheeler with bodywork after the style of a car and with doors, carpets, a roof, windows and outrigger wheels for stability at rest: remember the pre-war Whitcroft, built on these lines? But whatever it is to be, it will come, and we shall be released from the daft situation which confronts us at present'.

Extract from Avon News Sheet, September 1967:

'A computer programmer in Melksham, Wiltshire, owned a P50 with which he used to commute weekly to his home in Winterbourne, near Bristol. He took his car but it rode in the goods van of the train, the railway company charging him the child's fare for the car'.

Manx Star, 19th March 1982:

A report in the *Manx Star* of 19th March 1982 talked about the possibility of 'Peels being produced in Hull by Alan Evans who is said to have found a Peel gathering dust in Nottingham, taken it home in three carrier bags, and rebuilt it. Alan who was then 31 said, 'The Peel is just right for driving around town'. He was going to call the Hull produced vehicles 'The Bamby'.

Opposite: This fascinating drawings clearly indicates how Cyril Cannell put his initial thoughts onto paper. Despite the obvious changes to the design there are some interesting details already included. One wonders just how many thousands of such drawings were made?
(Manx National Heritage)

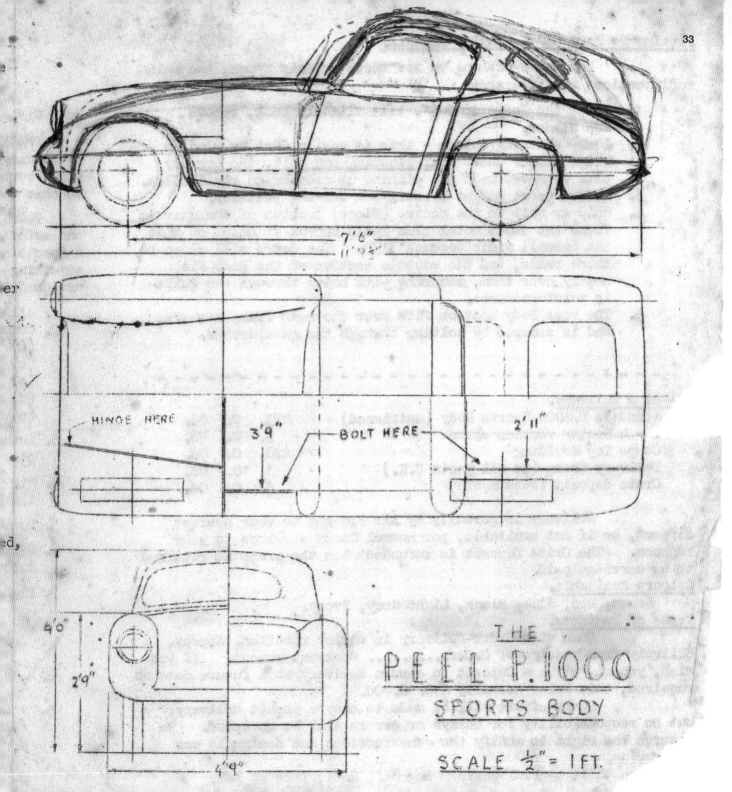

7' 6"

HINGE HERE

3' 9"

BOLT HERE

2' 11"

4' 0"

2' 9"

4' 9"

THE

PEEL P.1000

SPORTS BODY

SCALE ½" = 1 FT.

An advertising press picture of the underside of a P50. The minimal amount of metal is very evident. A small length of skirt has been removed to allow this picture to be taken. (Manx National Heritage)

Manx Star, 26th March 1982:

The *Manx Star* of 26th March 1982 had an article about the cars. It gave the weight as 112 lb and the designer as Cyril Cannell. Henry Kissack was the salesman of the organisation. Other engineers were George Gelling, Harold Murray and Ernie Leece. Miss Helen Cowell (Later Mrs Helen Costain) also assisted with the launch of the car at Earl's Court.

On one occasion Cliff Michelmore opened his television programme by actually driving into the studio in a P50. He commented that traffic experts had calculated that if everybody who travelled into London by bus or car all used a P50, there would be an 80% increase in the road capacity. Harold Murray took a P50 up in the lift of the Blackpool Tower, drove it round the balcony and brought it back down again!

One Peel owner who has both a P50 and a Trident in his collection commented that the engine numbers are only two apart, although the cars were probably built some 18 months apart, indicating that the DKW engines were probably stored and put into cars at random.

Research by Andrew Carter about P50 colours resulted in the following information:

Following my article on Peel colours last issue, several people have been in touch pointing out some mistakes. Thanks to Neil Hanson from the Isle of Man who sent me photocopies of 2 Peel advertising leaflets quite clearly showing the Trident available in Daytona White, Dragon Red, and Capri Blue. Plus the P50 available in the same 3 colours with the addition of Sunshine yellow. There is also a period photograph showing Peel Engineering sales manager Henry Kissack standing next to a new two-

It is almost possible to see the puzzled thoughts on the face of this gentleman. 'How am I going to get these 9 Tridents onto this trailer?' The cars were being loaded for their trip to the docks and delivery to dealers in England. (George Gelling)

A colorful line up.
(Barry Edwards)

The P50 prototype was, and indeed still is, unique and differed from the production version in many ways, most noticeable is the different wheel arrangement. The vehicle is seen here alongside Isle of Man Railways' brand new diesel locomotive No.21 at Douglas station on 1 August 2014. (Barry Edwards)

tone P50, (red lower half with white top).

It is a little confusing to me to see the P50 advertised as available in Capri Blue, as I had assumed (perhaps mistakenly) this was the light blue used on the Trident, not the darker blue usually seen on the early P50s.

Were there any pale blue P50s made? Or was this wishful thinking when printing the sales leaflets. Perhaps the secretary Helen Costain can still remember nearly 50 years later!

Thank you for all your comments - keep them coming.

Richard Lewis from the USA has sent me this picture of his P50 fitted with a single wheel PAV trailer. It might help Richard with stowing his shopping, but I'm not sure how safe it would be on corners or when braking from speed in the wet. Richard has travelled the whole of Route 66 in his P50.

The Trident

The P50 design was taken a stage further by Cyril Cannell, in 1965, when he came up with drawings for the one or two-seater Trident. The safety door gives unobstructed access. This vehicle was

An early promotional picture of
the interior of a P50.
(Manx National Heritage)

produced in at least four variations;

- Single Seater: a two-seater fitted with shopping basket
- Two Seater: Main production type.
- Automatic: One only completed
- Electric: One only completed

In common with the P50 and indeed all other Peel cars, the Trident had to comply with Vehicle Construction and Use Regulations.

The standard cars had the same power unit as the

P50 – a 49cc fan cooled two-stroke producing 4.2bhp with a petrol mix of 25:1, while the one automatic version had a 98cc engine. The vehicle had an enclosed chain final drive and three forward gears, steel wheels with 3.50 x 5 pneumatic tyres, with an internal parcel shelf over the back wheel instead of a boot, and was said to be less spacious inside than the P50! A two gallon separate fuel tank was installed on the nearside of the parcel shelf with a clear section enabling the eye to be used as a fuel gauge. The top end of the steering column was supported by the dashboard, the column then itself formed into the steering wheel. The steering wheel was designed to

Sam Knight and Chris Machin from the Manx Transport Heritage Museum in Peel proudly hold the commemorative banner after arrival at Port Erin. (Barry Edwards)

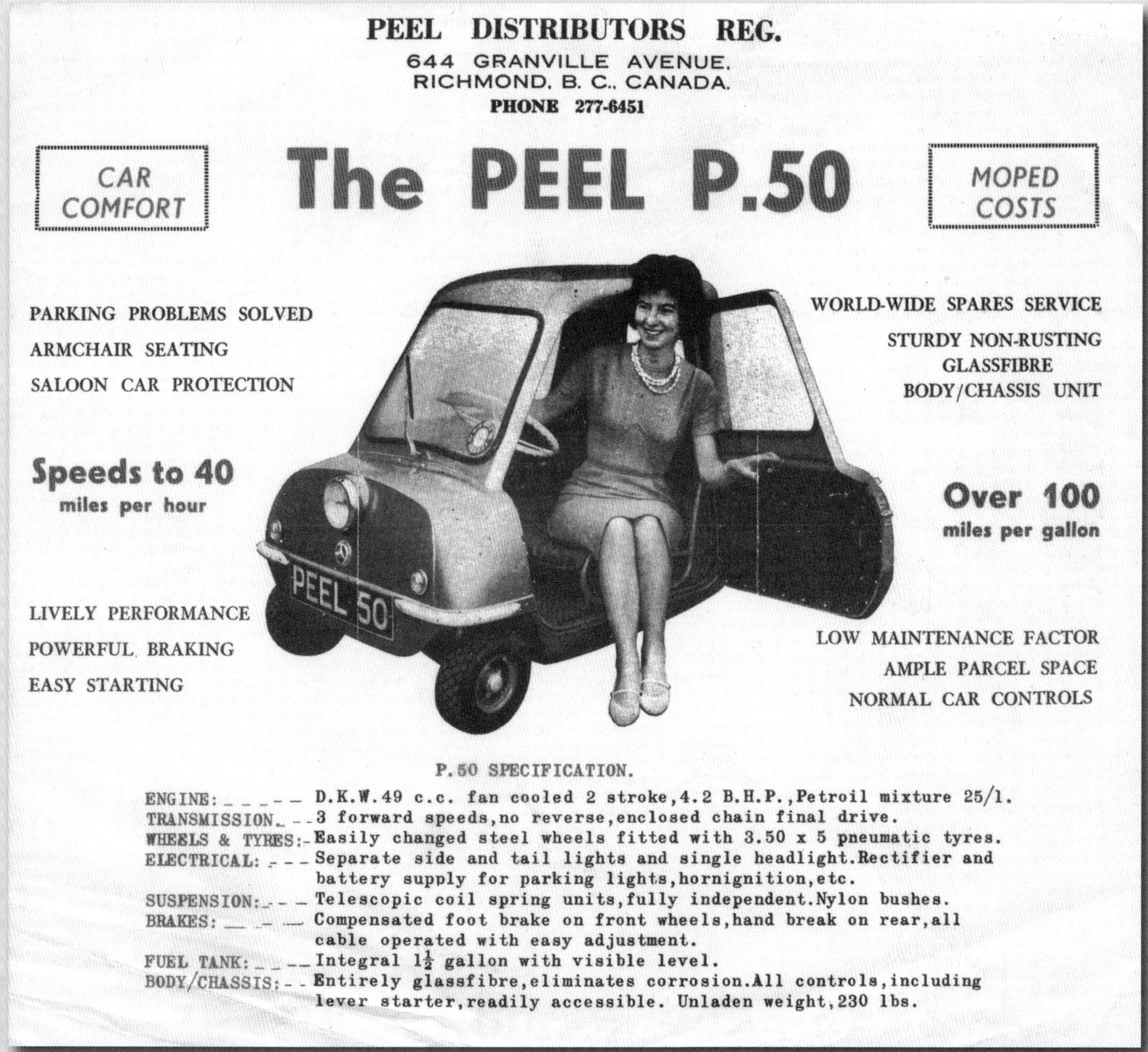

PEEL DISTRIBUTORS REG.
644 GRANVILLE AVENUE,
RICHMOND, B. C., CANADA.
PHONE 277-6451

CAR
COMFORT

The PEEL P.50

MOPED
COSTS

PARKING PROBLEMS SOLVED

ARMCHAIR SEATING

SALOON CAR PROTECTION

WORLD-WIDE SPARES SERVICE

STURDY NON-RUSTING
GLASSFIBRE
BODY/CHASSIS UNIT

Speeds to 40
miles per hour

Over 100
miles per gallon

LIVELY PERFORMANCE

POWERFUL BRAKING

EASY STARTING

LOW MAINTENANCE FACTOR

AMPLE PARCEL SPACE

NORMAL CAR CONTROLS

P.50 SPECIFICATION.

ENGINE: _ _ _ _ D.K.W. 49 c.c. fan cooled 2 stroke, 4.2 B.H.P., Petroil mixture 25/1.
TRANSMISSION: _ _ 3 forward speeds, no reverse, enclosed chain final drive.
WHEELS & TYRES: _ Easily changed steel wheels fitted with 3.50 x 5 pneumatic tyres.
ELECTRICAL: _ _ _ Separate side and tail lights and single headlight. Rectifier and
battery supply for parking lights, hornignition, etc.
SUSPENSION: _ _ _ Telescopic coil spring units, fully independent. Nylon bushes.
BRAKES: _ _ _ _ Compensated foot brake on front wheels, hand break on rear, all
cable operated with easy adjustment.
FUEL TANK: _ _ _ Integral $1\frac{1}{2}$ gallon with visible level.
BODY/CHASSIS: _ _ Entirely glassfibre, eliminates corrosion. All controls, including
lever starter, readily accessible. Unladen weight, 230 lbs.

A Canadian leaflet for the P50. (Grant Kearney Collection)

SOLVE YOUR PARKING PROBLEMS WITH

THE PEEL 'P-50'

After very extended tests, the 'P-50' is now being shown in production form. The designers feel that this vehicle meets the demands of thousands of buyers who require a vehicle offering the economy and convenience of a Scooter or small Motorcycle, with complete protection from the elements, and simple but adequate space for parcels, clothing, tools, etc.

Outstanding features are :

1. Easy starting mechanism, by hand lever conveniently situated inside car.
2. Adequate lighting provided, with switches easily reached.
3. Windshield Wiper and washer.
4. 'Intalok' Seating is rubber suspended, anatomically correct for persons of any stature.
5. Car type controls arranged in conventional position, clutch, brake, accelerator pedals, hand gear change.
6. Simple choke control with automatic 'OFF' device.
7. Lightweight but exceedingly strong Glassfibre Body/chassis unit of first quality materials built by Pioneers of Glassfibre Mouldings. Compact dimensions viz. 4' 4" x 3' 3" x 3' 10" height facilitate parking in the minimum space.
8. Detachable and interchangeable road wheels equipped with 'Avon' 350 x 5 tyres and tubes. No lubrication required to chassis, wheel bearings or control cables.
9. The robust Power Unit is of 'D.K.W.' manufacture — a 50 c.c. engine/gearbox unit providing over 4 b.h.p. This combined with 3 speed gearbox and multiplate Clutch (D.K.W.) provide ample power and speeds up to 35-40 m.p.h. with excellent petrol economy. 'Varley' Battery is charged by alternating current generator through rectifier unit . . . purpose being to provide ample road lighting and parking (which is by separate switch).

This vehicle has been run over the famous T.T. Course — the finest test in the world and has come out with flying colours. Yes ! it climbs up round the Gooseneck and Mountain Section very comfortably using its easily changed 3 speed gears.

Braking is effected on all 3 wheels by internal expanding brakes and parking handbrake is provided.

Provisional Price — including P.T. £199 10s. 0d.

The manufacturers reserve the right to alter the design and/or specifications at any time without prior notice. Deliveries will be made in strict rotation.   E. & O.E.

IT'S CHEAPER THAN WALKING

Manufactured by

Peel Engineering Co.

Viking Works, PEEL, ISLE OF MAN, G.B.
TELEPHONE: PEEL 590

Another of the many P50
leaflets. (Authors Collection)

A rare picture of a white P50,
known to have been sold to a
buyer on the Island by Peel
Engineering, and registered
9839MN. The picture was taken
at Maughold lighthouse on the
north east coast of the Island.
(Trevor Nall)

fold over in the case of impact and was copied from the Citroen DS19. A single switch on the dash board controlled the lights and dipper. The car had no electrical indicators although several reports suggest that a flasher unit would be easy to fit. Centrally mounted on the floor was the hand-operated starting lever, gear change and handbrake. There was no reverse gear. The vehicle was 6'0" long, 3'6" wide and 4'0" high and had an 8'0" turning circle and retailed at £189 19s 6d. The seat was simply moulded as part of the bodywork, the vehicle available in Daytona White, Dragon Red and Capri Blue.

The brakes, like the P50, were on the front wheels with the handbrake operating on the rear wheel. A lever starter was provided.

Trident parts were produced and supplied by:
- Windscreen: Clayton Wright
- Wheels/Hubs/Tyres/Brakes: Avon Cart Co.
- Head Lamps: Wico Pacy
- Rear Lamps: Stadium
- Switches: Lucas

A multi dealer P50 leaflet.
(Authors Collection)

Cyril Cannell and Henry Kissack with a P50 and its crate in the Showroom. The fact that the crate is strapped up would indicate that there is another car inside, ready for despatch. The vehicle on the right is of interest, it clearly has a two tone livery. (Manx National Heritage)

A few Tridents were fitted with a parcel shelf instead of the second seat. The shelf, made in fibreglass, was built over the seat after the main body had been moulded, ie, moulded as a two-seater and then modified. This was apparently to allow learner drivers to drive alone.

Like the P50s, each car was individually finished and so minor variations are likely between all the cars completed.

One car was fitted with the 98cc, 6.5hp engine and automatic transmission from a Triumph Tina motor scooter. This was a sample obtained from the Triumph Meridian Works. Triumph were sadly unable to supply sufficient engines to allow production cars to be fitted with them until about a year later, but that was too late for the Trident project. A Siba Dynastart was fitted to this car as an experiment, the idea was not repeated due to the cost and time involved.

The domes were produced in-house using a similar process to that developed to produce the windscreens for the fairings. The bubble was produced and then one side cut off and replaced by a flat plate of Perspex, the whole assembly was then re-heated to join the two parts together.

A 12-volt four-wheeled electric version with a CAV electric motor was built in 1966 and displayed at the Electrical Research Centre and also visited the Electric Drive Symposium in London. Cyril Cannell personally demonstrated this vehicle at the Symposium. Engineers from GEC later visited the Island to look at the vehicle.

The car was extensively tested around Peel but took 150amps to go up through the town; the area behind the back seat was crammed with lead acid batteries. This vehicle would have retailed at £190 0s 0d. Variations on quoted price include £189 19s 8d. This vehicle was sent to the English Electric Company and never returned.

A white Trident was delivered to ICI after being shown at a motorcycle show, the team at ICI were fascinated: how it was possible to blow a bubble with a flat on it?

Some extracts from a copy of a Trident Road Test Report by John A Cade.

This shows a price of £189 19s 6d and the distributor as Two-Strokes Ltd.

The tester was a man of over 6 feet tall, and remarks that even before getting into the car *'we already had the makings of a very funny situation'*.

The report continues: *'The Trident has no doors as such, the whole dome and front bodywork lifts up and forward giving easy access - looks rather like the gaping jaws of a crocodile. I settled myself in the driving seat and the Two-Strokes mechanic tried to fasten down the dome. Nothing doing, my knees were jammed against the dashboard. 'Try taking your coat off,' suggested the mechanic, trying to hide a snigger. Actually, this did help a little and I was away. However, no really large person could ever drive this vehicle in comfort.*

It is quite obvious that the Trident is designed for short runs to and from work or the station. Strictly a utility vehicle, the description 'Saloon Scooter' is just about right.

No Trafficators.

The standard model is not fitted with trafficators and I would regard these as practically essential. It

Gordon Fitzgerald's P50 sits snugly inside a VW camper van. This car has since been superbly restored and took part in the 50th anniversary celebrations in August 2014. (Gordon Fitzgerald)

The P50 in sunshine yellow. This colour was advertised on some promotional leaflets. Even at that size, it would be difficult to claim that you didn't see it! (Barry Edwards)

is none too easy making proper hand signals through the sliding panel provided. It would be a simple job to adjust the lighting to provide 'flashers'.

Petrol level is visible through a rather neat transparent panel'.

Fibreglass chassis

'The whole body and chassis unit is moulded in fibreglass so there is no danger of rust damage and the Trident is easy to keep neat and clean. It is fun to drive – a joy to park – easy on the pocket and very good value for £190. Used as a covered-in scooter for short daily trips to and from the office, the Trident should give long and useful service. However, it is not designed for holiday touring or for tall folk!'

Cyril Cannell said that it was a pity that a suitable UK made four-stroke engine was not available for both the P50 and Trident.

Archive footage of the Electric four-wheeled Peel Trident seen on Wallace & Gromit TV series.

Some things are hard to believe until you see them with your own eyes. In January 2011, Grant Kearney, a Peel car enthusiast, said he had heard rumours that the Electric four-wheeled Peel Trident had been seen on a new 'Wallace & Gromit's World of Invention' science series on BBC One.

There are several period black & white photographs of this one off prototype electric

A DKW 49cc engine removed from a car and restored to working condition. The special stand allows the engine to be run before refitting to the car. (Andrew Carter)

As part of the Isle of Man Vintage Transport Festival in 2013, the Manx Transport Heritage Museum P50 was taken by tram to the summit of Snaefell. The then 49 year old car is seen in the company of Snaefell Mountain railway car No.3, built by G. F. Milnes in 1895. Sadly the car cannot claim to have been up a mountain as although the summit of Snaefell is 2036 ft, the Tramway terminus is at just 1990ft above sea level. (Barry Edwards)

Opposite: Peel car collectors continue to stumble across original cars, many that have been stored away for years. One such example, discovered recently is shown here. It was restored and took part in the 50th anniversary celebrations on the island in August 2014. (Grant Kearney)

vehicle, however, film footage is exceedingly rare. A little detective work on the internet soon revealed the answer.

Episode 6 entitled 'From A to B', first shown on 8th December 2010, shows the Peel being driven somewhere in London.

Believed to be driving is Cyril Cannell himself, Peel Engineering owner and designer. The clip is only a few seconds in length, but a great piece of archive footage for Peel enthusiasts. The one-off Trident was designed with two rear wheels to cope with the extra weight of the lead acid batteries. The car had a removable rear panel to allow the batteries to be installed in the rear parcel area. The motor and switchgear were made by CAV. Reports of its performance were disappointing, poor range, slow and practically useless on hills. It was loaned to the University of British Columbia in Vancouver and

never returned to the Isle of Man. It probably remains somewhere in the University basement, so to all in BC Canada, it might be worth a little detective work to find this outstanding vehicle. Seeing this short film makes one wonder what else is hidden away in the BBC film library.

Danish Tridents?

After Peel Trident production ended in 1966, Cannell sold a set of Trident moulds, six Trident cars and a large amount of spares to a Norwegian entrepreneur who planned to re-start Trident production. Peel Engineering foreman George Gelling confirms this fact, but added that 'we had never been able to discover what had happened to the cars and parts'. Then, 'one day in 2009 a Peel Collector got an email from Denmark enquiring the price for six new Trident domes'.

This was a rather unusual request, but he tried not get too excited and asked for more information, with photos of the cars and parts. Several months went by without any further contact so it was assumed to be a wind up. Then, one day, a mind-blowing stream of pictures arrived by email showing cars, parts and spares (It turned out the owner did not have a digital camera and needed the help of her friend to email them). The pictures showed cars, boxes of new original parts, piles of wheels, cables drilling jigs etc. that proved beyond doubt that it was all genuine.

Upon further investigation, the purchase of a £45 air ticket was required in order to witness this discovery first-hand. To say that they had remained hidden for over 40 years was 'remarkable' is an understatement, (by chance it was the same week a Messerschmitt KR200 was discovered that had only done 47 miles from new). It turned out that some cars had been stored in different locations so it was difficult to determine exactly what remains elsewhere, but there were four complete cars (without Domes) 2 semi-assembled bodies with suspension, engines, and many boxes of new parts.

The parts have now been brought back to the UK and are stored in various locations in England and Scotland.

Mini Body

The Peel Viking was shown at a racing car show (sources suggest Olympia in London) where a Gentleman from Chile saw the car and proceeded to persuade BMC to make all the moulds and jigs, in order for Mini bodies to be built in Chile. The first bodies were made in Peel, the last small car body produced in Peel. As with the later Viking it used the mechanics and electrics of the factory supplied Mini. BMC Chilli was told by the Government that they had to make a percentage of the cars in the country and glass-fibre bodies were the cheapest way to do this.

A crash test was carried out on one of these bodies. It was driven into a concrete block at 30mph. While the front wings cracked, the bonnet

A sporty P50! This picture of a P50 cabriolet has recently come to light. Everything appears the same as other P50's, even the seat seems to be the original. The car would appear to be at some form of agricultural show. (Grant Kearney Collection)

came off, the boot lid opened and the petrol tank came out of its mounting clips, the main bulk of the car was unscathed.

These GRP Minis looked rather strange compared to the normal steel version, having no external seams, modified sills, wheel arches, rounded corners on the bonnet, and were slightly less curved inwards at the bottom to allow it to be released from the mould.

One prototype, chassis number 97, was used as a long-term test vehicle covering over 200,000 miles in 10 years. Company instructions were to 'try and break it'. Remarkably it has survived after BMC sold it to an ex-employee in 1982, who kept it for over 25 years in his garage. It is thought that only six bodies were actually produced.

BMC 1100 Body

Peel Engineering also produced two fibreglass BMC 1100 car bodies. Apparently BMC sent a man over to produce a set of jigs to allow the body to be drilled where fittings needed to be placed, however, the Peel engineers had put bushes into the mould in all the right places so that the holes were drilled before the body was removed from the mould!

Viking Sport

The Viking Sport body shell was designed to use the

Opposite: On the Sunday of the 2005 event, Island resident Sir Norman Wisdom O.B.E. joined the celebrations and took part in the cavalcade along Peel promenades as part of the Peel carnival. Trying a P50 for size, Sir Norman could not resist his show business style. This car was later purchased for the Manx Transport Heritage Museum. (Barry Edwards)

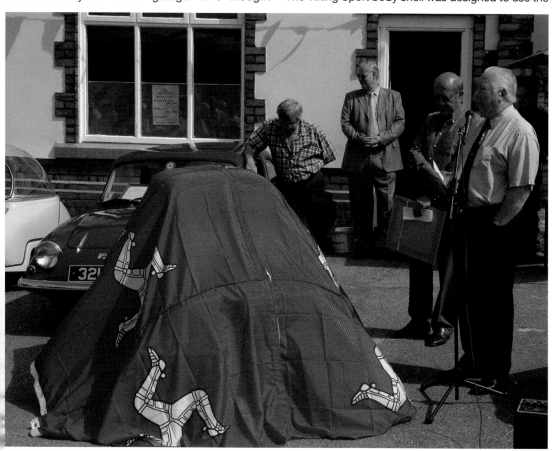

In late 2005 the Manx Transport Heritage Museum in Peel secured a P50 for its collection. The vehicle was purchased from the UK and collected from Liverpool by a group of members. Restoration began immediately and the car was completed by the middle of 2006. It officially launched, along with a set of stamps depicting the various Peel cars outside the Museum in July 2006. The Rt Hon Donald Gelling, the then Chief Minister of the Isle of Man prepares to pull the flag off the restored vehicle. (Barry Edwards)

Peel
Cars
28
ISLE OF
MAN
P50 MAN
'Peel P50'
Fusion Design
2006
Lowe-Martin
Peel
Cars
31
ISLE OF
MAN
'Trident'
Fusion Design
2006

mechanics and electrical systems from the BMC Minivan. The Minivan was chosen for its longer wheelbase. Everything from the Mini fitted into the Viking. The only additional part required was a longer speedometer cable, because the speedometer had been moved from its central position in the Mini to behind the Steering wheel in the Viking. A light steel tube frame was fitted internally and Known as the 'Bird cage'. The body retailed at £169 10s 0d.

Viking Performance Aids and Accessories for BMC Mini 850, 997, 998

Part No
VKM001: The complete Viking Sport Performance Kit for the above consists of:—

VM001: Polished or Green Crackled Alloy Rocker Cover.
VM002: Exchange Cylinder Head, ported and polished.
VM003: Carburettor Kit.
VM004: Straight through Silencer. Give Cooper performance to Standard Minis, with the single Carburettor, Cost £32 10s. 0d.

Left: Shortly after the unveiling of the car, a group of invited former Peel Engineering employees posed with the car. Many of these people speak fondly of working at Peel Engineering and are justly proud of what was achieved. (Barry Edwards)

Following the unveiling of the P50 for the Manx Transport Heritage Museum, three cars were driven through the streets of Peel to the Post office, where commemorative stamps were available. Being a Sunday the Post office was open specially. A number of people travelled by bus to the Post Office, the upper deck of the Leyland PD2 providing the vantage point for this picture. (Barry Edwards)

P50s are easy to transport and easily fit inside a Ford Connect van. The author actually moved two cars inside a normal wheelbase Transit. (Barry Edwards)

The Viking Sport Exchange Cylinder Head
VM002: Re-cut valves, relieved, matched flowed and polished. £22 10s 0d.

The Viking Twin 1½ S.U. Inlet Tract
VM011: With flowed exhaust tract, to replace single carb. £9 10s 0d.

The Viking Rocker Cover
VM001: Cast alloy superb polished finish or Green Crackle Absorbs engine noise, no distortion or oil leaks. £4 8s 0d.

The Viking Mini Organ Type Throttle Pedal Assy
VSM004: Dead smooth throttle opening through nylon cable. Pedal adjustable for rake. £3 5s 0d.

The Viking Mini Remote Control Gearchange
100% finish, superbly engineered.
VSM001: De-Luxe G.T. Model. £18 9s 6d.
VSM002: De-Luxe Model. £16 9s 6d.
VSM003: Standard Model. £13 9s 6d.

The Viking Polished Wooden Gearknobs
VM008: Various patterns and woods. 15s 0d.

The Viking Mini Stabilising Rod Kit
VSM007: Fits from gearbox to subframe, completely stabilising engine, and eliminating rock. £2 10s 0d.

The Viking Tachometer Cowling
Superbly hooded, fitting to steering column or dash to take the Smiths 8000 RPM electric impulse.
VM005: Tac. Finished in black crackle. £2 5s 0d.
VS001: Smith Tachometer for the above. £9 15s 0d.
VKM002: Both items purchased together. £11 0s 0d.
Note: Tachometer only required for Viking—Sport Body.

The Viking Wood- Alloy Steering Wheel
VM007: Superbly finished, authentic G.T. type steering wheel, specially produced for fitting to BMC Mini vehicle £7 10s 0d.

Wheel Spacers (for Mini range, Cooper rear not 'S' models) increases track to 1½" per axle, including high tensile studs. 39s 6d per pair.

Yacht Car

Another development, as the result of a request from a Channel Island millionaire who wanted a vehicle to carry four people with space for provisions, was for a car to fold as flat as possible and be able to be carried by two people. Looking something like a modern day golf kart, it had a fibreglass chassis, the Villiers light car 250cc engine fitted with Siba Dynastart that was mounted backwards behind the rear wheels driving through a sprocket chain. A fold-down roof that could carry the provisions and offer some protection from the elements was provided. A second was ordered and produced but it is not clear if any further examples were built.

This vehicle was eventually sold on 16th May 1974.

Go-Karts

Peel Engineering was also the pioneer of Go-Karting on the Island. The first karts were constructed with a 1½" steel tube frame, with a fibreglass pan and rear seat rest. They were powered by a Villiers 9E engine, had Ackerman rack and pinion steering and twin rear brakes. Later versions had a single brake in the middle of the rear axle. Geoff Duke did some

Pictures of the Go-Karts are rare, but this view has been found. It shows two Peel-built Karts in action at Onchan Stadium. The Karts were also raced on a circuit in Ballasalla. (Grant Kearney)

Karting comes with its own problems, so Peel Engineering took along their van with a repair kit! Trackside repairs are seen taking place here. One wonders how many it took to lift that gas bottle? (Grant Kearney)

test driving of the karts at Balthane Industrial Estate in Ballasalla. Some tests were also done on a circuit at Jurby.

A road-legal version was also produced, incorporating all necessary lights and mudguards. This was driven round the TT course by Ernie Leece, the only kart known to have to complete the circuit.

Later, a fuller bodied version was built, one was fitted with a 250cc engine while the majority had 175 or 197cc. Peel Engineering hired the Onchan track to run karting sessions, usually on Tuesday and Thursday nights, using various different versions of kart.

Accessories
The windscreen and bubble blowing box was also used to produce various accessories for other manufacturer's cars. Door pockets were produced for the Renault Dauphine and the two and four-door Morris Minor. These were formed from Polystyrene and were finished with a metal strip along the top edge. Rear wheel spats were also produced for the Dauphine.

A vehicle that really was way ahead of its time, was the electric Trident. The vehicle had 4 wheels to allow it to carry the weight of the batteries. It is seen here alongside other electric vehicles. (Manx National Heritage)

Amusement Film Show Machine
A development machine was produced to show a short film of a lap of Onchan Park kart track, using a loop of film with an ingenious system and a set of headphones. It was actually tested with a short film of the P50 climbing Peel Hill.

PARKING PROBLEMS SOLVED   ARMCHAIR SEATING

WORLD-WIDE SPARES SERVICE   SALOON CAR COMFORT

STURDY NON-RUSTING GLASSFIBRE BODY AND CHASSIS UNIT

ALL ROUND VISIBILITY

SAFETY DOOR GIVES UNOBSTRUCTED ACCESS

Colours available: Dragon Red, Capri Blue.

Dimensions: Length 6ft. 0ins. Overall width 3ft. 6ins. Height 4ft. 0ins.

Annual Tax: 3-Wheeler rate where applicable. Weight approx. 200 lbs.

SPECIFICATION

ENGINE—Fan cooled 2 stroke, 4·2 B.H.P. Petroil mixture 25:1. TRANSMISSION—3 forward speeds, no reverse, enclosed chain final drive. WHEELS AND TYRES—Easily changed steel wheels fitted with 3·50 x 5 pneumatic tyres. ELECTRICAL—Conventional lighting, Rectifier and battery supply for parking lights, horn, etc. Separate ignition system—easy starting even with flat battery. SUSPENSION—Telescopic coil spring units, fully independent. Nylon brushes. BRAKES—Compensated foot brake on front wheels, hand brake on rear, all cable operated with easy adjustment. FUEL TANK—2 gallon with visible level. BODY AND CHASSIS—Entirely glass fibre, eliminates corrosion, new improved design giving more interior space, visibility and engine accessibility. All controls including lever starter readily accessible. Compensated safety door allows parking in minimum space and cannot obstruct passing traffic.

DEALER

PEEL ENGINEERING LIMITED.

VIKING WORKS :: PEEL, ISLE OF MAN :: U.K.

These vehicles or components thereof are supplied with an express warranty, which excludes all warranties, conditions and liabilities whatsoever implied by Common Law, Statute or otherwise. PRICES:—The Company reserves the right to vary the list prices at any time. SPECIFICATION:—The Company reserves the right on the sale of any vehicle to make before delivery without notice any alteration to or departure from the specification, design or equipment detailed in this publication. Such alterations are likely to occur at any time.

7977/65.—Island Development Co. Ltd.

A Peel Engineering leaflet advertising the Trident. The reference to worldwide spares and the address shown for the Company indicate that sales were anticipated worldwide. (Authors Collection)

Opposite: The 4 wheeled Electric Trident on display with a number of other electric vehicles. The batteries are clearly visible housed where the engine would normally be. The car has the extra wheel in order to support the weight of the batteries. (Authors Collection)

Three Peels: two Tridents and a P50 stand outside Milntown House in the north of the Island. Parts of this historic house date from the 16th century, although the house as we see it today is substantially that completed in 1830 by the then Deemster John Christian. (Barry Edwards)

Model Boats

The company also produced a range of model speed boats and sailing boats and at least one model of a 25ft boat was made. These tended to be manufactured by the same team that made the fairings. Testing was carried out on a local lake, usually on Saturday afternoons.

The *Isle of Man Daily Times* reported in its issue dated 11th April 1961 that Peel Engineering had the consent of Peel Commissioners to use Mill Dam in Mill Road for operating small boats.

Viking Shields and Helmets

Another article in the Isle of Man Daily Times, issued 13th June 1961, describes the production of replica Viking shields and helmets for the Viking Festival to be held in the town on 4th July, being made at Peel Engineering.

Sea Terminal Building, Douglas, Isle of Man

Peel Engineering made and installed the spike on the top of the Sea Terminal Building in Douglas. After initial installation, George Gelling and Bill Gorry filled in all the fitting holes with fibreglass from scaffolding erected around the spike.

The Ford Prototype and Reliant Robin

The Ford motor Company produced a prototype car that appeared at the 1983 Geneva Motor Show. Known as the Ghia Trio the car was just 94.8" long and 53.6" wide. It sat the driver and two passengers in a triangle pattern, the driver sitting centrally at the front. The headlines at the time in the Manx press suggested that 'the P50 was 20 years ahead of its time'. The Reliant Robin also took some ideas from the Peel Engineering products.

Following a ceremony in Regent Street on 1 August 2014, a few of the cars were driven to the Steam Railway Station. Grant Kearney with partner Claire Naylor pass the Motorsport Merchandise shop, a shop that celebrates speeds that these little cars can only dream of, in his beautifully preserved Trident. (Barry Edwards)

A batch of 11 Tridents on-board one of the Isle of man Steam packet vessels, making the first part of their journey to Two Strokes in Stanmore Middlesex. (George Gelling)

The Seemeter

The Seemeter 300 was a machine tool direct reading measuring system. Developed by Cyril Cannell it attracted interest from a number of large companies, including Rolls Royce, but sadly never went into production.

Safer Steam Systems (IOM) Ltd, The Shipyard, Peel, Isle of Man.

This was a company name used for a new type of steam boiler that did not need to be pressure tested. The boiler had no tubes but square steel tubes with copper pipes inside. The heated steel bars in turn heated the copper but as no pressure was involved the boiler was not of the conventional type.

The Safer Steam Systems Company number was later used for Monasystems Ltd, during the development of a new monorail system, described later.

Trailers

Peel Engineering also produced around two-dozen trailers. These were about 4ft square and used P50/Trident wheels and suspension and had moulded fibreglass mudguards.

Stock Clearance

The following is copied from an original document showing items for sale by Peel Engineering. This document runs to several pages but the first page includes a number of interesting items:

STORE CLEARANCE GOODS FOR DISPOSAL
Prices in brackets (£...) show figure at which items were originally marketed. Clearance prices are in condition ex-store, carriage and packing to your address extra at cost. Terms of Business c.w.o.

SECTION 1 - Body Shells, Moulds, Development Vehicle Parts etc.

1. Sports car body shells, complete self-supporting type with lift-up bonnet, centre section with scuttle, double moulded doors with internal armrests, rear section with boot lid. Suit 7'6" wheelbase chassis, wheels up to 26" over tyre tread. (£85) £40.00

2. Hard top mouldings for the above (£25) £10.00

3. Experimental minimum single-seater vehicle, as exhibited at past Motorcycle show. Bodyshell and door only. £25.00

4. Jeep type 2 or 4 seater vehicle for petrol or electric propulsion, wheel size 16" x 14" overall size 87" x 48". GRP chassis pan mouldings only. £30.00

5. Mould to produce the above, well reinforced. Cost approx. £300-400. £75.00

6. Tubular steel front sub-frame for the above £5.00

7. Tubular steel rear sub-frame, electric drive model. £8.00

8. Components for electric drive model - 5 h.p. CAV traction motor, control gear, master switch, cooling blower, wiring harness etc. (£90) £35.00

9. Set of 4 new wheels, tyres, tubes, hubs for the above. (£32) £20.00

10. Chassis pans incorporating seats, luggage locker etc. as used for production 3-wheeler Trident

Good job it's small! A Peel Trident from the Lane Motor Museum in Nashville, Tennessee, USA is driven through the streets of Peel by Jeff lane from the Museum, with Maureen Knight as a passenger. The car had been shipped from the USA specially for the event. (Barry Edwards)

Saloon Scooter. (£25) £12.50

11. GRP body mouldings for the above (front hinging) (£20) £10.00

12. Prototype BMC type Mini bodyshell in GRP with doors, boot lid, bonnet etc. one only £150.00

13. Mould to produce the above, with metal frame and trunnion mountings. Offers invited.

14. New metal BMC 'Mini' bodyshell, used only for pattern work, needs cleaning and tidying, otherwise complete and sound. (£85) £50.00

15. Tubular steel space frame chassis for advanced 'wedge' style vehicle, to accept either Renault or BMC Mini mechanical components, with optional rear or mid-engine layout. Aircraft type sliding canopy, steeply raked windscreen etc.

At present fitted with Renault mechanical parts for sizing and initial test purposes. Cost in the region of several hundred pounds. £125.00

Monasystems Ltd, Monorail

Although not actually produced under the Peel Engineering banner, Cyril Cannell's revolutionary design for a monorail is worthy of inclusion here. It shows that despite being technically retired, Cyril continued to research, design, and indeed produce models of new ideas. The prototype of the monorail is currently in storage and will become an exhibit at the Jurby Transport Museum in due course.

The re-instatement of the former Isle of Man

Opposite: A general view of a Manx registered Viking, restored to brilliant condition and often driven around the Island. (Barry Edwards)

A Trident Dome before fitting to a car. This is actually a replica produced in exactly the same way as the original ones. (Andrew Carter)

Railway line from Douglas to Peel has been discussed many times. Meanwhile, Cannell had designed and patented in 2005 a new type of Monorail (patent number: GB2401089B) that could be erected quickly to provide a much needed rail link to the west of the Island. Cannell described his plans:

'The first railway built on the Island to carry passengers was that from Douglas to Peel, this about 40 years after the early ones in England, but with a mainly fishing and farming industry the need here was obviously less urgent than for the Industrial Revolution taking place over there. However, the Island did chalk up an important first in the electric railway built from Douglas to Groudle, the very short and marginally earlier one on the beach at Brighton being only a novelty tourist attraction.

Nowadays, Peel is the only sizable town here not to have a rail link to the capital; this is even more regrettable in having much poorer road access than the others when the main direct one is closed for racing. Relaying of the original surface railway line today would be not practically possible, but not so for an elevated system, which would not be hampered by road crossings, newly installed infrastructure or changes of ownership of the land. The exact location of an ideal new route would of course be the province of the relevant authorities and surveyors, but the line could readily serve the new hospital and Onchan. Possibly extension in the future to Kirk Michael, Ballaugh and even the forthcoming developments at Jurby.

The new elevated railway now proposed is of the Monorail type and almost certainly the quietest, lowest cost and most quickly erected 'go anywhere' system of any, and could be mainly constructed by local engineering firms. With traction equivalent to 'rack and pinion' railways, the line could run at ground level to minimize adverse visual impact, but climb and descend where necessary to surmount obstacles or for boarding. Patents are involved, but as this would be the first full size version built, not only in the British Isles but also the rest of the World, only one half of the normal user licence fee would be accepted. This project would bring long-term and worthwhile benefits to Peel, especially with the increasing population and congested roads. It can come to fruition if enough people voice their approval. An express line linking the railway terminals in London using this system has been proposed, but there is no reason why Peel and the Island should not be first'.

The system was promoted as the 'Future Tramway and Light Rail Transit' the system that offers affordability in manufacture and in land space occupation, and would be quicker to build than virtually any other system.

Other advantages are as follows:-

- It need not occupy already over-congested road space, it can be located over pavements in town or city areas, or confined to existing transport pathways.
- Most environmentally friendly, 'whisper quiet' and may be elevated or at ground level as required to minimise visual impact.
- Not affected by strong side winds as almost all other systems are, including conventional railways.
- Can readily traverse valleys and rivers, a truly 'go anywhere' system.
- 100% adhesion for traction, so able to climb and descend for passenger access in short distances, or to surmount road junctions or other obstacles.
- Severe weather capability and simple automatic monitoring of rail integrity.

Following the development of the fibreglass Mini body, Peel produced a fibreglass Morris 1100. Seen here sporting one of the three Peel Engineering 'Trade' plates MNA192. (George Gelling)

- Built in 'Tilting Train' provision, and compact single-stantion supporting structure.
- Low mounted power units, with space underneath, gives good servicing access.

The prototype of the monorail is currently in storage and will become an exhibit at the Jurby Transport Museum in due course.

New Peel models.

A new limited edition 1:32 scale Peel P50 collectors' model is now available. Made in metal, highly detailed with chromed fittings, it is available in red, blue and kit form, larger than the now discontinued 1:43 S.A.M.S model at 46mm in length. The P50 is the first in a range to be offered by model makers ARC Microcars, with the Trident to follow soon.

An interesting dual coloured Viking, that would appear to be at some kind of show. One wonders if the owner found a buyer?
(Grant Kearney Collection)

Four of the Peel factory workers pose with a completed Viking with the showroom building in the background. The Trojan motor van with registration 768MN is hiding behind the building. (George Gelling)

A complete Viking body as it would have emerged from the factory. The doors have yet to be fitted and a coat of paint applied. Then all that is required is a Mini chassis.
(Andrew Carter)

Another view of the completed Viking body shell. Evidence of filler and sanding to complete the joints is visible forward of the front wheel arch.
(Andrew Carter)

Peel Owners have their say...

Peel Experience

I first saw a Peel Car at the Burford Microcar rally in the mid 1970s. It was a blue Trident, and had several adults and children crowding around it staring in amazement. A few years later, Messerschmitt owner Mark Smith took me to visit Malcolm Goldsworthy in Kent who at the time had a wonderful collection of old cars including 4 Peels. From that moment on I was enthralled by these amazing little cars. We left Malcolm's farm towing a Peel P50 tied to the back bumper of Mark's Ford Fiesta, using a bit of old rope around the rear handle of the Peel, and I remember seeing it skipping along backwards at speeds of 70mph+ through the rear window. In 1984, my wife and I drove from Hamburg to Hannover, Germany, in a Peel Trident, and I remember how incredibly hot it was under that dome.

In 2007, Jeremy Clarkson from BBC2's Top Gear asked if he could borrow my Peel P50 EME 583B to use in their show.

Initially I was rather apprehensive about loaning the Peel, however I was allowed to follow the film crew around all day, as long as I promised to stay out of shot behind the cameras. Filming started at 6.00 pm prompt and I was immediately put at ease by how friendly and professional the whole team were. I was impressed that Jeremy Clarkson was

BMC put one of the fibreglass Mini bodies through a crash test. It was driven at a concrete block at 30mph. The very limited damage is clearly evident in this view taken shortly after the test was completed.
(Manx National Heritage)

genuinely interested in the Peel – he asked many questions and drove it very skilfully. His on-screen bravado and arrogance were not evident in real life, and I had a great time watching the filming. Jeremy obviously enjoyed driving the Peel, describing it as being way ahead of its time: 'I have seen the future, and it comes from 1964'.

Those 9 minutes of the Top Gear program have become one of the most popular clips in the history of the show.

Over the years I have visited Peel on the Isle of Man several times, and have always received such a warm and friendly welcome from Peel Engineering employees Ernie Leece and George Gelling, and Sam Knight from the Manx Transport Heritage Museum.

For all the Peel's shortcomings, Cyril Cannell aimed to design a cheap local runabout, and in my mind he was a very successful engineer - way ahead of his time. Who would have guessed 50 years ago how sought after these tiny cars would become.

Andy Carter, Nottinghamshire.

Nearly caused a divorce!

You may remember that my late husband owned a P50 and a Trident which myself and my son Andrew brought over to Peel for the last gathering, I am afraid I shall not be able attend this time but at least one, maybe both cars, will be with you. They are now owned by my grandsons so one of the dad's will have to come too.

I well remember when Edwin first acquired the Peels in the very early 1980s, each for the princely sum of £300. The P.50 came first and was duly restored in-house by Edwin, even down to the spraying, no cheque book restorations in those days. We took it over to the Story Rally in Germany in 1981, where it took part in the road run in the Hartz mountains and appeared on German TV, the first Peel ever to do so I believe. The Trident was a different story, it was being used to store garden tools when Edwin found it, and its dome had a large

piece missing from it, and when I found out he had paid £300 for such a wreck it nearly caused a divorce!!! Those were the days when you could have fun with your cars, not treat them as investments.

Jean Hammond, Kent.

An apPEELing Drive

Every drive in our Peel Trident or Peel P50 is a memorable one. Rarely seen on public roads in the United States, onlookers are simply amazed. I do want to share one of my funniest experiences in the Peel P50.

Lane Motor Museum has been fortunate to have a car on display every year at the Amelia Island Concours d'Elegance. About six years ago, they decided to host a Microcar Class, and we were invited to bring our Peel P50. On Friday before the show, there was a car tour that I enjoy participating in. It is about 40 miles long, and I figured I could do it in the P50. I asked at the beginning of the tour if there was any interstate driving on the route. The organizers said no, so off I went, starting at the back so I would not hold up the group. Most of the time, I could drive in the bike lane and not hold up traffic. About 15 miles into the tour it appeared I was entering a freeway, and sure enough, there I was, driving on a 4-lane freeway to go over the Intracoastal Waterway in Jacksonville, Florida. I figured I had to just keep going because I was following directions, and if I got off the route I would be lost. Plus, the shoulder was very wide, and I could drive on it, staying out of everyone's way. Half way up the bridge, I saw construction ahead. The shoulder and two right lanes were closed... 'oh no!' I couldn't turn around so I pressed on, and at least one other lane was open so others could pass by me. That theory did not work too well, as every car that came up next to me slowed down to take a picture. Fortunately, the bridge is only about two miles long, and I was soon back on the 2-lane road.

I finished the rally with about three hours driving time, and can tell you, three hours in a Peel P50 is

As well as performing a crash test, BMC also tested a fibreglass Mini body for rigidity. Interestingly, it proved to be slightly more rigid that its metal counterpart. (Manx National Heritage)

a long day! It was worth it though, as almost everyone you see along the way is smiling and gives you the thumbs up.

Jeff Lane,
Lane Motor Museum, Nashville, Tennessee

Malcolm and Sheila Thomas's Adventures in the Peel Trident

My interest in Peels started in the mid 1970s when Tony Marshall and myself started collecting Microcars under the name of The Surrey Microcar Collection. We managed to acquire 3 models, the light blue Peel Trident, a dark blue P50 and a red single seater (shopping) Trident. At that time we found quite a few other Peel P50s and Tridents, but were not able to afford most of them, however, we found other enthusiasts to save them.

The Peel Trident was manufactured on the Isle of Man by Peel Engineering Ltd. It has a 49cc DKW moped engine, 3 forward gears and no reverse. Its vital statistics are: 1.05m wide by 1.80m long by 1.25m high.

We awoke on the morning of Thursday 22nd August 1987 at 6.30. The sun was shining and the birds were singing. This was our big day – a test of skill and endurance: to drive, two-up and with full camping gear, in a fully restored Peel Trident, to the

Some of the larger manufacturing work was carried out at Jurby, inside one of the former RAF hangars. Here we see two workers moving one of the BMC Mini bodies, with apparent ease. There appears to be another mini body behind and one of the smaller boat hulls in the foreground. (Manx National Heritage)

A completed Mini with fibreglass body, the slight differences are clear, notably the shaping round the top of the wheel arches and along the bottom of the body. (Grant Kearney)

Another view of the complete Mini. Interestingly left hand drive for the Chile market. (Grant Kearney)

Dutch Micro-car Rally at Bergambacht, approximately 100 miles (as the Peel drives) from Vlissingen Port in Holland and 60 miles for our home in Purley to Sheerness.

We checked our sense of humour and luckily it was in good form. At 9.00 we had a photocall on the lawn. We piled all the things we were going to take in front of the Peel and set the camera to automatic so we could both be in the picture. It was difficult to see how all the gear was going to fit in with two people as well, but in fact it packed in beautifully with a little room to spare.

At 9.45 we set off on our adventure – at 9.47, 200 metres from our back gate, we had to stop to get rid of the wasp that was flying around inside the dome! And as it was already hot inside the car we stripped off our tracksuits down to shorts and T-shirts which thrilled the main road motorists!

If you have ever sat inside a metre cube sized greenhouse with a friend (we still were at this stage) with no windows open you will know exactly what the Peel Trident is like on a hot and sunny day!

We raced along, up and down the highways and byways of England, topping, probably (no speedo), 35 mph at some stages, down to 5 mph in 1st gear up hills but never once having to stop and push. After an hour and a half we stopped to stretch our legs and bring our bottoms back to life.

As we approached Maidstone we were overtaken by Malcolm Goldsworthy – known to many of us and another Peel owner – who just happened to be in the area. At midday we arrived sweating buckets at the Studios of Southern Television. TVS were planning to have a group of Micro-cars on a Saturday morning children's programme called 'No.73' scheduled for 26th September. We lunched with the researcher and discussed ideas for the show.

We left the studios at 2.00pm and were faced with about a three-mile-long steep hill. We took a run at it and although we soon slowed down into 1st gear the Peel kept going – no trouble. Before reaching Sheerness Docks we stopped to deface a signboard, showing a silhouette of a boat with a lorry and a car inside, indicating the way to the ferry terminal. By cutting out of paper the shape of the Peel we were able to stick this in the front hold of the boat and take some photographs with the 'big' Peel parked alongside the sign.

We arrived at Sheerness six hours before the Olau boat was due to sail! (Well, we didn't know the journey was going to be so easy!) We were hot but not bothered. It was very interesting to hear peoples comments as they passed the Peel' such as 'it's not a real car'; 'you can't' get two people in that' (oh yes you can), 'it's a Messerschmitt', 'a Bond', 'how do you get in it'; 'I bet it gets hot in there' (not 'alf); etc, etc.

We were first on to the boat and as Olau charged us full car rate we wanted as much space as a Rolls Royce or Volvo, and made sure we weren't squeezed into some odd corner.

At 7.15am next morning we drove off the boat and were in Holland, and as navigator I produced the first of the three maps we would have to use to go the 100 miles to the rally site. The maps were very kindly sent to us by Sjoerd ter Berg and were large-scale cycling maps. We had plotted our route with a marker so I knew where we were headed, using a combination of cycle paths, parallel roads, and very occasionally a main road.

We planned to go over the Zeeland Bridge which is approx. 5km long, on the cycle path which we found without difficulty. Half way across we saw in the distance what looked like something blocking the way. As we approached we could see some vans and men working on the bridge and there was no way we were going to get past. We both got out and Malcolm lifted the back and turned the Peel around and back we went to try and get across on the major road. The cycle path was toll free but on the main route there were toll booths and a special three-wheeler rate. The man collecting the tolls was not very happy to let us across because we could not reach, let alone maintain, a minimum speed of 70km, but we told him the cycle track was blocked and he let us go over. So after crossing the bridge nearly 3 times we continued on our set route. We saw parts of Holland we had never seen before and it was very interesting to see all the little villages with cobbled streets (!) and of course, open fields and windmills.

20km before Schoonhoven we spotted a lovely windmill which was more a thatched cottage with a windmill grafted on the top, and as it was another very hot day we needed some air, so we pulled up in front of it and took some photographs. Then Malcolm felt the tyres to see how hot they had become and not only did he find them hot but the

front two were completely bald! And after only 200 miles! We drove to the nearest telephone (no mobiles in those days) and rang Harry Rutgers, the only Peel Trident owner in Holland, to arrange some replacement tyres.

At 2.00pm we arrived at 'De Nes' campsite Bergambacht, which had a very steep road leading

The sole surviving Peel Yacht Car came to the Island for the celebrations in August 2014. It is captured here, still needing a few parts to complete its restoration but at least it survives. (Barry Edwards)

off the dyke. It was extremely hot by this time – even outside the car. We put up our tent and unpacked the other camping gear. Some people couldn't believe that we had driven from England and across Holland in such a vehicle.

That evening a barbecue had been arranged for us all and we were all supplied with a large variety of meat to barbecue ourselves, salads and French bread, all washed down with an ample supply of beer.

On Saturday morning Malcolm changed the front tyres and measured their depth before we set off on the 45 mile sightseeing trip. The tour was very interesting. Our first stop was at Molens Kinderdijk, a series of 19 windmills used in the 18th century to drain the west part of the Alblassenwaard. This is now done by an enormous pumping engine. It poured with rain, so donning our wet weather gear we went around the windmills. The second stop was Streekmuseum Krimpen a/d Ijssel which showed how the Dutch lived years ago. A very enthusiastic man was there who was keen to tell us, in perfect English, all about the exhibits. There was a special exhibition of private collections, which included a collection of thimbles which was fascinating for me being the proud owner of approximately 200 thimbles myself.

When we returned to the campsite, Malcolm measured the depth of tread again and after just 4 miles there was significant wear. With help from Pete van de Poll they improvised a way to test the tracking and it was way out. So it was adjusted until it was approximately correct. Then Malcolm decided to add a shim to the steering to eliminate the play, but he couldn't get the shim in in time for dinner and no way was Malcolm going to miss his dinner! He put the steering column back without the shim.

We left for Lekkerkerk at 6.30pm and lined up on the dyke road so that we could travel in convoy to the restaurant. When we arrived we filled the car park and people climbed on builders' equipment to get 'aerial' views and photographs of the cars. We had a very nice but extremely spaced out meal. In between the main course and dessert Henk Tappel, on behalf of DWAC, presented us with a lovely memento of our trip made by Nico Krap – a marble

One of the many internal fittings produced by Peel Engineering, were these fish van interiors, designed to protect the inside of vehicles. The fibreglass also provided a good surface for the storage of fish, and was easy to keep clean. (George Gelling)

slab illustrated in black with 'The Greatest Idiots come in the Smallest Cars' and then a very accurate drawing of the Peel Trident buzzing along – a wonderful gift for something that in fact turned out to be a relatively easy and practical trip! After dinner two films were shown, brought all the way by Peel Trident, of the 1984 Rally at Drouwen and the 1985 Rally at Berkhout; then a video taken at last year's Rally at Henxel. We drove back to the campsite with the Peel's big beams lighting our way.

Malcolm rose at some unearthly hour on Sunday morning and put a shim in the steering, after dropping it in the long grass and having half a dozen people looking for it. We went in convoy to Schoonhoven and parked in the car park next to the Ferry. All cars taking part in the fuel economy test were set up and had two thirds of a litre of petrol in a special plastic bottle. The Peel only came 4th because it was running rich, it was two-up and the bottle seemed to leak when we turned it upside down (excuses, excuses). Pete van der Poll, in his Messerschmitt, and a Heinkel both got back to the campsite with petrol to spare.

An 'unusual' lunch followed, consisting of pancakes cooked on a gas griddle served with syrup and sugar and milk. We had some heavy downpours of rain during this and the rest of the afternoon. Henk made his 'End of Rally' speech in three languages at 4.00pm and the Rally was over for another year.

As it was very hot again on the Monday, Malcolm

One of the many vehicle accessories manufactured by the
Company were these door pockets for the Renault Dauphine car.
(Manx National Heritage)

The actual mould used to produce the door pockets is cleaned ready for use. The lettering that appears raised on the finished product is clearly visible. (Manx National Heritage)

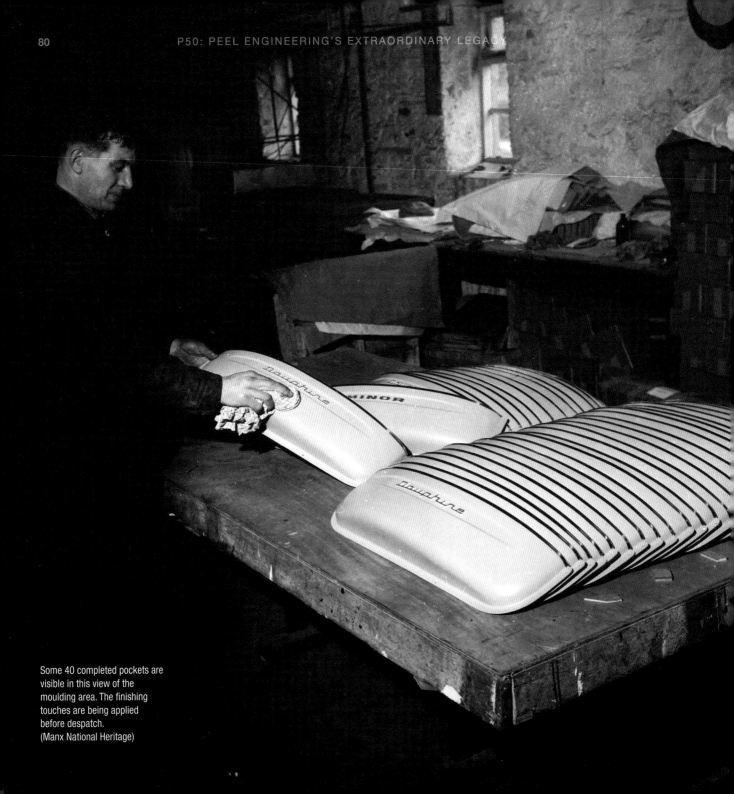

Some 40 completed pockets are visible in this view of the moulding area. The finishing touches are being applied before despatch.
(Manx National Heritage)

decided we really needed an air conditioning system for our homeward journey, so he retrieved a plastic carton from the rubbish which he connected by means of tape and wires to the ventilation hole on the car. As we drove home it was great because it was hot outside and we were cold inside. Then the weather deteriorated and we had to put on more clothes to keep warm, then the wetter weather gear because it started to rain!

We went back more or less the same route. We crossed the 5km bridge all the way on the cycle track and reached Vlissingen safely. The sea was very rough and although the Olau boat is usually rock-steady it wasn't quite so smooth. At 3.30 in the morning Malcolm decided to check that the Peel was alright (and presumably wasn't being seasick!)

In England it was pouring with rain and every time a lorry passed us it was as if someone had thrown a bucket of water through the air conditioning de-mist system! We tried blocking the hole but after 100 metres we couldn't see a thing for mist, so Malcolm got wet but visibility was great! We arrived home at 11.00 on Tuesday morning.

We must thank the organisers of the Rally – Hielke Dijkstra and Jaap Monster – for an extremely enjoyable, smoothly run, Rally; also Henk Tappel (Chairman of DWAC and multi-linguist); Harry and Irene Rutgers for the superb service of tyre deliveries; Pete van der Poll for equipment and tracking help; Sjoerd ter Berg for sending us the maps, and of course Nico Krap for the wonderful plaque and finally just everyone at the Rally for their company and friendship.

Now what can we go in next year...

Sheila Thomas, Surrey

The final event of the 50th anniversary weekend saw the cars take their place in the 2014 Peel Carnival. After a brief technical hitch with a flat tyre, some of the cars are seen on Peel Promenade with Peel Castle as a backdrop. (Barry Edwards)

Following behind the Peel P50s in the Carnival procession were the Tridents. (Barry Edwards)

Following the Carnival procession, the Peel cars returned to the Museum car park by driving back along the procession route. Here two local Police officers look on in amazement. (Barry Edwards)

On a short detour! One of the Trident cars tries out the footbridge for size. (Barry Edwards)

Employees Reminisce...

The recent event to commemorate the 50th anniversary of the Peel 50 and Trident production provided the opportunity to chat with three former employees. Celia Joughin, Helen Costain and Edith Hutsforth shared some memories.

They clearly enjoyed their time at Peel Engineering although commenting that it was hard work, 8.00am start until 5.00pm finish with a lunch and two short tea breaks. In common with many today, they described the pay as 'low', starting at 14 years of age on £1/0/0 per week in around 1958, rising to £1/10/0 at the ripe age of 15 years.

Former workshop foreman George Gelling described the trio as 'The finest fibreglass laminators in the world' and the girls felt they could still do it today. They recalled that their clothes would eventually stand up on their own as they inevitably became covered in resin.

The TT and Grand Prix Festivals were very busy times for the company with many visitors, other than those actually racing, visiting the company to have a Peel Fairing fitted to their Motorbike. The team often worked until 9.00pm to get fairings fitted to bikes.

The group well remember working deep inside the front of the 35 foot boat produced by the company. There was no real ventilation inside the hull so a commercial vacuum was used to suck out the fumes. This process was used in a number of similar situations.

They also recalled a number of 'off factory' work carried out by the company, The College and Empress Hotel Swimming Pools that required a special resin to prevent damage from chlorine. The Sulby Filtration Plant, a large water tank on Snaefell Summit, the spike on top of the Sea Terminal building, the Cross on the front of the Methodist Church on Loch Promenade that had a metallic gel coat, a plating tank at Ronaldsway Aircraft Company, again with a special resin to resist plating acid, two chimney stacks in Crosby and the gas tanks on South Quay.

The girls stated that they were 'Never allowed in the cars for testing!' Indeed one employee commented that her first trip in a car was in a Trident visiting the Island for a rally in 2005, the car had come all the way from the United States!

Perhaps the most notable thought was that when they were busy making the fairings and cars, little did they realise that 50 years on, the products they had manufactured would be still in existence, let alone be collectors' pieces changing hands for significant sums of money and having the 50th anniversary of their production celebrated in such style.

An interesting display of cars adjacent to the factory on 3 August 2014. (Andrew Carter)

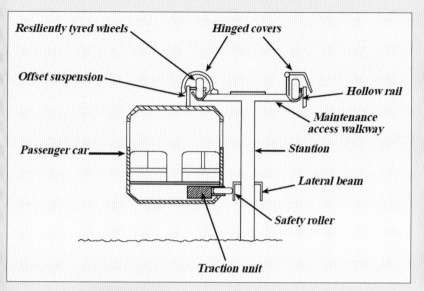

Resiliently tyred wheels

Hinged covers

Offset suspension

Hollow rail

Maintenance access walkway

Passenger car

Stantion

Lateral beam

Safety roller

Traction unit

Left: A general layout drawing of the proposed Monorail. (Authors Collection)

Above: An artists impression of Cyril's monorail somewhere between Douglas and Peel. The line would have followed the Isle of Man Railway route, opened originally in 1873 and closed in 1968. The route is now a public footpath that would not bedisrupted by the installation of the monorail. (Authors Collection)

PEEL ENGINEERING

MANX HOVER VEHIC PEEL ENGINEERING

Left: An interesting picture of the Hovercraft, taken at some form of show, describes it as a 'Hover vehicle' and claims that it 'Travels 3 feet off the surface'. (Trevor Nall)

Miles Cowsill, the publisher of this book, envisaged a cover picture of a P50 taken alongside an Easyjet A319 aircraft at Ronaldsway Airport. With agreement from both Easyjet and the IOM Airport management, the Manx Transport Heritage Museum P50 was taken out and photographed alongside the, by comparison, massive A319. The car is captured sitting in front of one of the aircraft's CFM56-5B5/P jet engines. The aircraft is G-EZAU, c/n 2795. (Barry Edwards)

Another view of the tiny P50 alongside Easyjet A319, G-EZAU at Ronaldsway. (Barry Edwards)

On Friday 1 August 2014 a short ceremony was held outside the Douglas Post office in Regent Street, to launch a limited edition First Day Cover marking the 50th anniversary of the production of the Peel cars. Despite the inclement weather, a good turn out of cars was matched by large crowds. Here we see some of the owners standing beside their cars. (Barry Edwards)

Isle of Man Stamps
Cowraghyn Post Ellan Vannin

MANX STAMP & COIN NEWS

Midsummer 2006 No. 113

Peel Cars

P·50 MAN

Also in this Manx Stamp & Coin News... Peel Cars • Manx Links With Washington • Queen Elizabeth II 80th Birthday Special Folder • Manx Bird Atlas & Belgica Sheetlet • IOM Post Year Collections • Harry Potter Collectibles • Isle of Man TT 2007 • IOM Sportsman Special FDC • A History of IOM Coins • QEII 80th Birthday Crown Coins • The IOM Treasury Coin Collection and much more...

The front cover of the Manx Stamp and Coin News from Summer 2006, coinciding with the launch of the Peel Car stamps and the inauguration of the P50 for the Manx Transport Heritage Museum in Peel. (Authors Collection/Isle of Man Post Office)

On Friday 1 August 2014, seven Peel cars including the prototype P50 were loaded onto a flat wagon and taken by train to Port Erin as part of the 11.50 departure from Douglas. The train formed part of the celebration to mark 50 years since the cars were produced and 140 years since the railway between Douglas and Port Erin was officially opened. The various owners are seen strapping the cars down in a view taken from the cab of locomotive No.21. (Barry Edwards)

The 'Motorail' train is seen passing Keristal between Douglas and Port Soderick, with locomotive No.21 driven by the Director of Public Transport Ian Longworth in charge. Steam in the form of No.4 Loch was used to bank the train throughout its journey. (Barry Edwards)

As part of the celebrations in August 2014, a number of cars were intending to complete a lap of the world famous Isle of Man TT course. Sadly the weather soon put a stop to that idea but, late in the day the cloud cleared and two cars did complete a lap. Here we see Grant Kearney guiding his Trident round 'The Gooseneck' as he climbs up out of Ramsey. The TT riders complete the 37.75 miles in something just over 17 minutes, the current record holder is Bruce Anstey with a time of 17 minutes 6.682 seconds, an average speed of 132.298mph, riding a BA Honda CBR1000RR. (Barry Edwards)

THE
'SEEMETER 300'
(Patents Applied for)

Machine Tool
Direct Reading
Measurement System

•

SAVES TIME, MATERIAL MONEY

SIMPLE – PRACTICAL
LOW COST

The SEEMETER 300 is a piece of equipment specifically designed to save you time and money and to increase the profitability or your workforce and equipment. It enables the Machine Operator to measure diameter or thickness directly without stopping the machine, also simplifying and reducing time spent in setting and checking the workpiece for truth. At a price of only a fraction of electronic DR systems, every relevant machine in your factory or workshop may be equipped and the very moderate outlay quickly recovered.

Installation of the SEEMETER 300 equipment is very simple. Accuracy checks may be quickly made, the complication of multi-tooling and cutter wear inherent with other systems are eliminated.

SPECIFICATION — SEEMETER 300

Suitable for lathes from 3″ centre height upwards, all sizes of milling and shaping machines. Measurement normally up to 6″ diameter external and internal (minimum practical bore size 1½″ diameter, contact bearings for bores to ½″ diameter to order). Thickness to 3″. Direct measurement reading to 0.0005″. Alternative metric unit if required.

Foot pedal operated, measurement probe with large area grease lubricated adjustable bearing surfaces. Probe mounting by conveniently arranged clamp, with self-locating action on reference bar, provision also made for slide or machine frame mounting. Cable and pedal systems mechanically and ergonomically designed to equalize contact pressures and to deter overloading.

ALL WEARING PARTS REPLACEABLE AT LOW COST

Manufactured by—

PEEL ENGINEERING LIMITED
VIKING WORKS, PEEL, ISLE OF MAN
TELEPHONE ——— STD 0624 84 2590

The Manufacturers reserve the right to pursue their policy of constant improvement and to alter and amend the specification at any time without notice.

Norris Modern Press Ltd., 6 Victoria Street, Douglas, Isle of Man

A self explanatory leaflet.
(Authors Collection)

One of the many official press pictures of the Trident, taken alongside the River Neb in Peel. (Manx National Heritage)

Appendix 1: Peel production vehicle quantities and colours.
This interesting table is reproduced by kind permission of Andrew Carter.

Vehicle Type	Peel P50	Peel Trident
Years built	Oct. 1963 to Dec. 1964	Dec. 1964 to Dec. 1966
Total estimated production.	55	86
Cars known to still exist.	28	33
Records held of cars not known.	5	6
Total records held.	33	39
Standard colours.	Red, Blue, White.	Red, Pale Blue.
Colour data of recorded cars.	Red 19 (58%)	Red 29 (74%)
	Blue 9 (27%)	Pale Blue 10 (26%)
	White 4 (12%)	
	Yellow 1 (3%)	

Appendix 2:
Peel Built Vehicles known to have carried Manx Registrations

Registration	Date Registered	Previous Registration	Previous Registered	Date Registration	Current Registered	Date Type	Vehicle Number	Engine Number	Chassis	Notes
9504MN	28th March 1964	L80MAN		P50MAN		P50 White	80416004683	D539		
9694MN	17th April 1964					P50 Blue	80416004965	D525		Later sold to Two-Strokes in Stanmore and registered HMP612B
9759MN	23rd April 1964					P50 White	80416004754	E102		Engine now in America fitted to a Trident.
9759MN	27th October 1964					Trident Red				
9759MN	3rd January 1965					Trident Red				
9839MN	7th May 1964					P50 White	80416004731	D524		Registration Documents show colour as White
UMN10	17th Sept 1955					Manxcar Red	10	10		Registration Cancelled 1st October 1962
UMN945	30th May 1956	Chassis or original vehicle MAN498			28th August 1935	Peel 1000	RY7425178	107186		Body only from Peel, Chassis 8hp Ford
723BMN	9th Feb 1965					Trident Red	80416004728	E126		Under restoration in Scotland
209DMN	16th August 1965, cancelled 30th August 1967					Trident Red	8041	E153		Sold twice by Raymotors, 2nd time on 8th July 1966, Shipped to UK and re-registered HCM719F
151GMN	17th Oct 1966, Cancelled 17th Feb 1970	9028JZ	June 1965	MAN123	9th Oct 1981	Trident Red	80416004673	E148		Registered new in Northern Ireland, Transferred to IOM, back to NI and then back to IOM. Also appears to have been P656MAN, 3rd September 1981
MAN66P	17th April 1967	357EMN	24th Feb 1966, cancelled 8th Sept 1966			Viking Red	GFD-SH244			Exported as 357EMN, returned and registered MAN66P
MAN 321A	January 1989	MAN100W	9th May 1978	321MAN		Viking Red	Minisport 0908			The MAN321A registration was changed to 321MAN for a short while
MNA190						-	-	-		Trade Plates
MNA191						-	-	-		Trade Plates
MNA192						-	-	-		Trade Plates

Appendix 3:

Dealers in the UK known to have supplied Peel Cars

- Two Strokes Ltd, Church Road, Stanmore, Middlesex. A consignment of 12 cars was shipped by the Steam Packet to this dealer.
- Goodfellows of Walsall, Walsall Rd, Aldridge, Walsall, West Midlands.
- Three Crowns of Aldridge, Sutton Road, Aldridge, Walsall, were advertising Peel cars in the December 1964 issue of *Garage News*.
- Kings of Oxford, Oxford Road, Kidlington, Oxford.
- H. Petty & Sons, Motor Engineers, Highfield Street, Leicester.
- H.E. Bridge, Stanley Road, Bootle, Merseyside.
- Life's Motors Ltd, West Street, Southport, Merseyside.
- Bosworth & Carvell, Bank Street, Rugby, Warwickshire.
- Allens Motors (Bacup) Ltd, Central Garage, Burnley Road, Bacup, Lancashire.
- Glen Henderson Motorcyles, Heathfield Road, Ayr, Scotland.
- W Searing Motorcycles, Basbow Lane, Bishops Stortford, Hertfordshire.
- W G Tiliston of Stockton-on-Tees, known to have sold chassis numbers E134 and E136.
- Wilson & Cannavan of Killinchy, Co Down.
- Browns of Witham.

The beautifully restored P50 belonging to Gordon Fitzgerald complete with its 'Short Vehicle' sticker in the rear window. (Gordon Fitzgerald)